THE HOLY KAUW COMPANY

Road Trip Cooking

Arno & Mireille van Elst

Hardie Grant

TRAVEL

Let the journey begin!

For us, road trips represent a roaring engine, long roads, majestic views, good conversations and loud singalongs to guilty pleasures blaring on the radio; pulling over when we see something beautiful, when we are hungry or just because we need a break from driving; then unwinding and enjoying the simple things in life: being in the great outdoors, lighting a campfire or going on a mission to find the best local produce. But they also mean making friends, cooking together, sharing meals and, above all, learning new things and gaining inspiration.

Whether you're travelling through outback Australia, road tripping through the English countryside or camping in the mountains or by a forest lake, cooking and enjoying scrumptious meals is possible anytime and anywhere.

In this book we will show you how you can make tasty and nutritious meals in a simple way, even when you don't have a fully equipped kitchen or a well-stocked supermarket nearby. We outline various outdoor cooking techniques and include both simple recipes and recipes that require a bit more time and effort. We hope these tips and hacks will make your outdoor cooking experience even more fun!

Let the journey begin!

Mireille & Arno
The Holy Kauw Company

Contents

Road trip hacks

When you're on the road it's best not to bring too much stuff, so we've put together some road trip hacks that will make cooking fun and easy.

GOOD THINGS COME IN SMALL PACKAGES

Sugar, salt and pepper, mustard, little jars of jams, small tubs of butter and refresher wipes – if you know you are going on a road trip, it's handy to bring them along, but these are things you can leave behind on your road stops when you're finished with them. This way you have seasoning on hand without having to drag heavy pots and packs along. The same goes for small packets of soy sauce, wasabi and ginger; these are ideal for life on the road!

LIGHTWEIGHT HERBS AND SPICES

We like cooking with herbs, so to avoid carrying too much we have collected little lip balm containers, toothpick holders and sweet tins so we can store small amounts of dried herbs and spices in them and take them on our trip.

SLEEPING BAG FOR A TEA COSY

Do you need to prepare several dishes on a single fire? Keep whatever is cooked first warm inside a sleeping bag. It's also a great way to warm your bed on a cool night – put a pot with the lid on, kettle with hot water or teapot in your sleeping bag for a wonderfully pre-heated sleeping place!

WASHING BAG FOR A STRAINER

A washing bag works very well for draining rice, pasta or vegetables. And it takes up very little room.

SLEEPING MAT FOR A COOLING ELEMENT

Keep items cool by placing them under your sleeping mat when you sleep in a tent. Tents heat up quickly, but temperatures stay lower under the sleeping mat as the ground is cooler and isolated under the mat. This way you can keep wine, butter and chunks of cheese nice and cool. Don't forget to check you've removed all the food before going to sleep.

ROCK FOR A PESTLE

A big rock and a tree stump work perfectly as a pestle and mortar. Crush garlic, mix spices or crack open nuts. Make sure the rock and tree stump are free from sand and grit.

ROCK FOR A GRILL
You can cook pork belly to a perfect crisp on a stone by the fire. The same probably goes for eggs, but we haven't tried that.

Cooking on the road

While on the road we cook with practical items and techniques. Take the time to make a fire, build a barbecue or have the charcoal reach the right temperature. Slow cooking your meals makes your food even tastier. An added bonus: it makes you incredibly zen!

FIRE
Nothing is more enjoyable than making a good fire. You can hang a pot off a campfire tripod, bake potatoes and vegetables, melt marshmallows on a stick and cook an egg in a paper bag. A fire is also a great way to stay warm on colder nights.

Some tips:
+ Always check you are allowed to have an open fire at the campsite. Not only because you risk getting a fine but also because it can be outright dangerous.
+ Always keep a jerry can with water on standby when you're having an open fire.
+ Put out the fire when you go to sleep or hit the road. Respect nature and the environment and leave things as you found them.

BARBECUE
When preparing food on a barbecue, make sure you wait until the charcoal reaches the right temperature before you start cooking. If you don't have a barbecue lid, you can place a bigger pan upside down on top of the qrill and cover the food that way.

DUTCH OVEN
A cast-iron pan is heavy and not the most practical item for on the road, but we consider it essential. You can use this cast-iron friend for virtually anything. We bake bread with it, and make stews and soups in it. We also use it to make omelettes or bake potatoes. You can put a Dutch oven directly on the charcoal/in the fire, and you can play with the temperature by varying how much charcoal or wood you use under it or on top of the lid.

COOKING INSIDE A TIN
An empty tin can be used to heat up food or you can even bake bread in it. This can be a fun activity to do with the kids and different from cooking bread on a stick. You can also boil water inside a tin, but watch out for the sharp edges.

COOKING ON YOUR ENGINE
It's really possible! Wrap the food, place it on the engine block and drive off to your next destination. By the time you reach your next stop, it will be ready.

How amazing is that? When you drive, the engine reaches around 90°C (194°F) – this heat is perfect for cooking. It's important to find out where the hot spot of the engine block is. The best way to find out is to touch different parts of the engine with a damp/wet finger after a long drive. Cooking on an engine block is safe, does not smell and does not damage your car. Make sure you use enough aluminium foil when wrapping food and that it is tightly wrapped so no moisture or fat can escape. Avoid using too much liquid or fat to prevent leakage. One last tip: it's a good idea to use gloves and tongs to pick up the hot parcel from the engine.

SINGLE BURNER STOVE

Not just for making coffee or heating up a tin of soup, the single burner stove can be used to cook great recipes. We make one-pot meals with it and, if we need to use more pans, we keep the food warm by placing the pan in a sleeping bag. It's all about thinking outside the box.

Packing list

You get the idea, you don't need a lot to put a good meal on the table, but we always take the following items with us:

+ Box of matches. We keep these in different places because it's possible for leaks to appear after a downpour, right where you keep the matches! So it's better to be safe than sorry.
+ Charcoal (not briquettes)
+ Sharp chef's knife
+ Chopping board
+ Aluminium foil, an absolute MUST for your outdoor kitchen. You can keep meals warm with it but we also use it to build mini-ovens.
+ Survival pocket knife (complete with a tin can opener)
+ Jerrycan with clean water. Refill at every stop. You really don't want to run out.
+ Lightweight pans

+ Wooden spoon
+ Grater
+ String
+ Duct tape. Everything can be fixed or solved with this fantastic roll of tape. Lifesaver number one when on the road.
+ Wooden pegs, just as multifunctional as duct tape. You can use them to close packets, hold a small light, tie neatly rolled cables and rope, clamp your sunglasses to your sun visor, clamp it to the wooden spoon while cooking so it doesn't slide into the pan, and so on.
+ Gloves to move hot pots and parcels from the fire. Also handy for wild picking.
+ Tongs to pick up smouldering charcoal and wood, and to turn over the food on the fire.
+ Rubber bands to close packets and keep things bound together.
+ Paper bags to pack lunch, to bake eggs in (see p. 12) and to use as a bin bag.
+ Steel wire brush or steel wool to keep the barbecue grill clean.
+ Coffee percolator because, oh boy, even on holiday, you can't start your day without a coffee!

Preparation time

The preparation time for meals prepared outdoors is difficult to determine with exact precision. It is dependent on a number of things like weather conditions, the time it takes to start a decent campfire and get the barbecue going and, of course, the actual temperature of the fire or barbecue. That's why we provide only a rough idea of cooking times. (This does not include the times for lighting a campfire or barbecue.)

Numbers tell the story

As there are usually no cooking scales on the road, we use our hands, cups, tablespoons, teaspoons and pinches. Use common sense and follow your gut feeling, and you can't go wrong. Taste is very personal, so if you have a sweet tooth, use more sugar than is indicated. Just make sure you think about the balance of flavours; it needs to stay tasty. If you're not sure of the measurements, add small quantities and keep tasting. It's better to add a little than too much, which could ruin the dish. For those who prefer to work with exact measurements, see the table below.

Ingredient	1 teaspoon	2 teaspoons
water	5 ml (⅛ fl oz)	10 ml (¼ fl oz)
baking powder	5 g (⅛ oz)	9 g (¼ oz)
flour	3 g (⅛ oz)	5 g (⅛ oz)
butter	5 g (⅛ oz)	10 g (¼ oz)
cacao powder	3 g (⅛ oz)	5 g (⅛ oz)
lemon juice	5 ml (⅛ fl oz)	10 ml (¼ fl oz)
honey	7 g (⅙ oz)	14 g (½ oz)
milk	5 ml (⅛ fl oz)	10 ml (¼ fl oz)
oil	4 ml (⅛ fl oz)	9 ml (¼ fl oz)
sugar	4 g (⅛ oz)	8 g (¼ oz)
salt	6 g (⅛ oz)	12 g (¼ oz)

Ingredient	1 tablespoon	2 tablespoons	3 tablespoons	4 tablespoons
water	15 ml (1/2 fl oz)	30 ml (1 fl oz)	45 ml (1½ fl oz)	60 ml (2 fl oz)
baking powder	14 g (1/2 oz)	28 g (1 oz)	42 g (1½ oz)	56 g (2 oz)
flour	8 g (1/4 oz)	16 g (½ oz)	24 g (1 oz)	32 g (1½ oz)
butter	15 g (1/2 oz)	30 g (1 oz)	44 g (1½ oz)	58 g (2 oz)
cacao powder	8 g (1/4 oz)	16 g (½ oz)	24 g (1 oz)	32 g (1½ oz)
lemon juice	15 ml (1/2 fl oz)	30 ml (1 fl oz)	46 ml (1½ fl oz)	61 ml (2 fl oz)
honey	22 g (3/4 oz)	43 g (1½ oz)	65 g (2¼ oz)	86 g (3 oz)
milk	15 ml (1/2 fl oz)	30 ml (1 fl oz)	46 ml (1½ fl oz)	61 ml (2 fl oz)
oil	13 ml ½ fl oz)	27 ml (¾ fl oz)	40 ml (1¼ fl oz)	53 ml (1¾ fl oz)
sugar	13 g (1/2 oz)	25 g (1 oz)	38 g (1½ oz)	51 g (1¾ oz)
salt	18 g (3/4 oz)	36 g (1¼ oz)	53 g (2 oz)	71 g (2½ oz)

A pinch is the quantity that fits between your thumb and index finger. A handful is a small fistful as opposed to a bucket-load.

Life is better off-road

Waking up to the birds. Drinking coffee by the fire. Getting freshly baked bread from the local bakery. Baking eggs. Good morning world, where are we going today?

Paper-bag breakfast

AN EGG FROM A PAPER BAG!

» FIRE » PREPARATION LESS THAN ½ HOUR » SERVES 2 » BREAKFAST

INGREDIENTS
+ 100 g (3½ oz) bacon, in slices
+ 4 eggs
+ curry powder
+ salt and pepper

EQUIPMENT
+ 2 paper bags
+ 2 twigs

Baking eggs in a paper bag: I never would have believed it if we hadn't tried it for ourselves. Combine all of the ingredients in a bag, pierced with a twig at the top and you're all set. Hang it above a smouldering wood fire and after five minutes the egg is cooked and the bacon is mostly crispy.

METHOD

1 Make a good campfire.

2 Line the slices of bacon side by side inside the bottom of the paper bags. The fat from the bacon will keep the bags from catching fire.

3 Carefully crack open two eggs into each bag and sprinkle with curry powder, salt and pepper (don't overdo it with the salt as the bacon is naturally salty).

4 Carefully roll the bags shut and puncture a hole at the top of the bag so you can stick a twig through.

5 Hang above a fire until the eggs are cooked. This should take approximately five to eight minutes.

✽ Note: don't beat the eggs with milk. The mixture will get too moist and the bag may leak.

Spiced porridge
WITH NUT MIX

» **FIRE** » **PREPARATION LESS THAN ½ HOUR** » **SERVES 2** » **BREAKFAST**

INGREDIENTS
+ 450 ml (15 fl oz / 2 cups) milk
+ 5 tbsp (70 g / ⅓ cup) oatmeal
+ 200 g (7 oz / 1 cup) grated carrot
  (2 medium-sized carrots)
+ 1 tsp (5 g / ⅛ oz) cinnamon
+ 1 tsp (5 g / ⅛ oz) ginger powder
+ 1 tbsp (15 g / ½ oz) peanut butter
+ maple syrup, to taste
+ 1 tbsp (15 g / ½ oz) mulberries
  or raisins
+ 30 g (1 oz / ¼ cup) mixed nuts,
  roughly chopped (or use a rock to crush)

Waking up in the morning, going for a refreshing dip in the lake and returning to the campfire, shivering with cold. How good is it to warm up by the fire with a bowl of steaming porridge? This version looks like a little cake – so good! At the same time it's super healthy and nutritious. If you prepare the oatmeal before your dip in the lake, it will be the perfect temperature when you get out. Just make sure someone keeps an eye on the fire.

METHOD

1 Add milk to a small saucepan and bring to the boil. Stir in the oats.

2 Simmer gently for five minutes and keep stirring. Add the carrots and spices and simmer until the carrot is soft.

3 Turn off the heat and leave the lid on the saucepan for approximately five minutes.

4 Pour into two serving bowls. Add a bit of peanut butter and a drizzle of maple syrup. Top with nuts and mulberries.

❉ You can stir in more warm milk to thin the porridge.

Come, have breakfast!

WITH RICE, MANGO AND CASHEWS

» FIRE » PREPARATION LESS THAN ½ HOUR » SERVES 2 » BREAKFAST

INGREDIENTS
+ 1 cup short-grain rice
+ 200 ml (7 fl oz / 1 cup) coconut milk
+ 1 tbsp (22 ml / ¾ fl oz) maple syrup
+ pinch of cinnamon
+ pinch of salt

+ 1 ripe mango, sliced
+ 2 tbsp (30 g / 1 oz) chopped cashews
+ 2 tbsp (30 g / 1 oz) shredded coconut
+ zest of ½ lime

This breakfast bowl is perfect to warm up on a chilly morning. It will keep you full for hours.

METHOD

1 Rinse the rice and then boil in the coconut milk. Keep stirring and make sure the rice doesn't burn on the bottom of the pot. Add a bit of water if the mixture gets too dry.

2 Stir in the maple syrup, cinnamon and salt, and pour into two serving bowls. Top with mango, nuts, shredded coconut and lime zest.

✱ You can add anything to your bowl. We prefer this rice when it's colder outside because we like to have this as a warm meal, but you can also use yoghurt as a base and use different toppings. Some tasty combinations are:

+ *toasted muesli, banana, peanut butter and chocolate*
+ *puffed quinoa, blueberries and honey*
+ *toasted oats, stone fruit, maple syrup and vanilla*
+ *strawberries, mint and balsamic vinegar*

TIP
Stir in a spoonful of peanut butter
for a more filling breakfast.

It can take a while before the bread is ready, so don't start making the dough when you're already hungry; nobody likes a grumpy camper.

Bread from a tin

» DUTCH OVEN » PREPARATION IS OVER 1 HOUR » SERVES 4 » BREAKFAST

INGREDIENTS
+ 1 pack of bread mix and the ingredients needed as indicated on the bread-mix packet
+ olive oil
+ 2 tbsp (30 g / 1 oz) oat flakes or bran

EQUIPMENT
+ 2 clean and empty tins

Keep yesterday's empty bean stew tin to bake bread the next day. Of course it's fun to make bread dough from scratch, but when you're on the road it can be tricky to find some of the ingredients – there's no shame in using a bread mix.

METHOD

1 Make a fire and wait until it smoulders so you can put the Dutch oven on it.

2 Make the dough according to the instructions on the bread-mix packet. Knead the dough so it's smooth and elastic.

3 Grease the inside of the tins using the olive oil – be careful not to cut yourself as the edges may be sharp.

4 Make two small rolls from the dough, big enough to fit in the tins.

5 Use a spoonful of oats to dust the inside of each tin. This will help the bread come out more easily once it's baked.

6 Place the dough in the tins. Cover with a tea towel and leave dough to rise for 10 minutes. Place the Dutch oven on the bed of coals to pre-heat.

7 Put the tins inside the Dutch oven, cover with a lid and leave the bread to bake for about 40 minutes.

✳ You can also use this technique with a barbecue. Heat to approximately 180°C (355°F) and cover with a lid or place a pan upside down over the tins. Serve with homemade jam or a local cheese.

If it involves mountains, breakfast, coffee or campfires, I'm in.

Forest fruit feast

WITH CARAMEL AND CAKE

» FIRE » PREPARATION IS LONGER THAN ½ HOUR » SERVES 2 » BREAKFAST

INGREDIENTS
+ 300 g (10½ oz / 1½ cups) mixed forest fruit (strawberries, raspberries, blueberries)
+ 1 tbsp (13 g / ½ oz) brown sugar
+ 1 tsp (5 g / ⅛ oz) butter
+ 2 thick slices of butter cake, cut into cubes
+ 1 chocolate caramel bar, cut into cubes
+ 1 tbsp (15 g / ½ oz) chopped walnuts

Truly finger-licking good! The best part about this cake is using your own hand-picked fruit. Using store-bought fruit is totally fine too.

METHOD

1 Make a fire and place a grill on top, or light the barbecue.

2 Add the fruit and sugar in a bowl, stir to combine and leave to stand for a couple of minutes.

3 Melt the butter in a cast-iron frying pan and fry the cubes of cake until brown. Turn regularly.

4 Sprinkle the fruit evenly over the cake cubes and place the chocolate bar between the cubes. Cover the pan with aluminium foil and leave chocolate to melt for approximately five minutes.

5 Top with chopped walnuts before serving.

6 Eat as is or add a dollop of yoghurt.

✱ You can also use other fruit for this recipe. When using apples and pears it will take a bit longer to cook until they are soft.

TIP
Use a big rock to crush nuts or to crumble a biscuit. Place the ingredients on a chopping board, cover with a clean tea towel and crush to get your desired texture.

Warm peaches

WITH CREAM AND INSTANT CRUMBLE

» **FIRE/BARBECUE** » **PREPARATION IS LONGER THAN ½ HOUR** » **SERVES 2** » **BREAKFAST**

INGREDIENTS
+ 250 ml (8½ fl oz / 1 cup) cream, or 400 ml (13½ oz / 1½ cups) thick yoghurt
+ 4 ripe peaches
+ 1 tbsp (15 g / ½ oz) butter
+ 4 plain sugar biscuits (or other), crumbled
+ handful of toasted and chopped walnuts or almonds
+ 1 tsp (5 g / ⅛ oz) cinnamon, spice mix or five-spice powder
+ 1 tbsp (22 ml / ¾ fl oz) maple syrup

Scenic views, a steaming mug of fresh coffee and some peaches with cream and crumble. It doesn't get much better than that on the road. You can substitute the cream for yoghurt if you want something healthier.

METHOD

1 Make a fire or light the barbecue.

2 Whip the cream until peaks form and divide into four bowls.

3 Halve the peaches and remove the stones (pits). Warm the butter in a cast-iron pan above the fire and fry the peaches until they are dark and soft.

4 Mix the biscuit crumb with the nuts and spices.

5 Add the maple syrup to the pan just before the peaches are done. Distribute the peaches evenly on the cream and sprinkle with the crumble. Pour the warm butter and maple syrup from the pan over each bowl.

✱ You can also use canned peaches or peaches from a jar. In this case you won't need maple syrup. Canned peaches are already sweet enough because they're preserved in syrup.

Orange coffee

INGREDIENTS
+ 2 oranges
+ 2 instant coffee bags
+ boiling water
+ sugar (optional)

Orange and coffee are powerful taste friends. Have this fragrant coffee if you need a warm pick-me-up. Use the orange pulp from the hollowed-out orange in a salad or a breakfast bowl.

METHOD

1 Slice a small piece off the bottom of each orange so it stands up on its own (this will be used as your 'coffee cup').

2 Slice off the top, carefully scoop out the pulp and hollow out each orange with a sharp knife.

3 Add an instant coffee bag to each orange and pour in the boiling water. Stir in a tiny bit of sugar if you like sweet coffee.

✳ Extra options for more flavour:

+ *a pinch of cinnamon*
+ *1 tbsp (22 ml / ¾ fl oz) ginger syrup or crushed cardamom peel*
+ *a bit of rum and brown sugar*

TIP:
Is hollowing out an orange too much of a hassle? In that case just add orange rind to the coffee in the filterbag.

Do you feel more like savoury bread? Substitute the carrot for a zucchini (courgette) and use grated cheese instead of cinnamon and raisins.

Carrot bread
FROM THE DUTCH OVEN

» **DUTCH OVEN** » **PREPARATION IS LONGER THAN ½ HOUR**
» **MAKES 1 LOAF OF BREAD** » **BREAKFAST**

INGREDIENTS

+ 250 g (9 oz / just over 1 cup) butter
  (reserve 50 g / 2 oz for serving)
+ 3 eggs
+ 200 g (7 oz / 1 cup) brown sugar
+ 200 g (7 oz / 1 cup) grated carrot
+ 100 g (3½ oz / ½ cup) white raisins

+ 50 g (2 oz / ¼ cup) walnuts, chopped
  (you can also use pecans or pistachios)
+ 200 g (7 oz / 1 cup) flour
+ 1 tsp (5 g / ⅛ oz) baking powder
+ pinch of salt
+ pinch of cinnamon

This recipe is great because you can get carrots almost anywhere and freshly baked bread smells delightful. Make a fire and off you go! Also nice to take on a hike in the mountains.

METHOD

1 Make a fire and wait for it to smoulder.

2 Melt 200 g (7 oz / just under 1 cup) of the butter in a pan.
Beat the eggs in a bowl and stir in sugar and melted butter.

3 Add the carrot, raisins and nuts and give it a good stir.

4 In another bowl, add the dry ingredients and knead the egg–carrot mixture.

5 Pour the batter in a Dutch oven and cover with the lid. Place in the fire and leave
the bread to bake for approximately 40 minutes. Use a sharp knife to check
if the bread is done. If the blade comes out clean, the bread is ready.

6 Leave the loaf to cool down. Cut into thick slices and spread with
a generous amount of butter.

✳ With the bread that's leftover (if you're able to resist eating it all at once)
you can make delicious French toast the next day (see p. 34).

Breakfast burritos

FILLED WITH AVOCADO AND TOMATO

» FIRE » PREPARATION IS LESS THAN ½ HOUR » SERVES 2 » BREAKFAST

INGREDIENTS
+ 2 wraps
+ 4 eggs
+ splash of milk
+ salt and pepper
+ olive oil
+ 1 avocado, diced

+ handful of cherry tomatoes, halved
+ 1 large tbsp (20 g / ¾ oz) sour cream
+ pinch of cayenne pepper
+ lime juice
+ 1 tbsp (15 g / ½ oz) chopped coriander (cilantro) or flat-leaf parsley

Quick, tasty, nutritious and healthy. A great start to the morning when you've got a long day on the road ahead. You can use any type of filling for these wraps – use what you've got left lying around so you don't have to carry it to your next destination, or make up your own version with your favourite ingredients. This recipe is just one option.

METHOD

1 Briefly heat up the wraps in a dry frying pan above the fire.

2 Mix the eggs with the milk, salt and pepper in a bowl.

3 Heat the oil in a frying pan and pour the egg mix in. Lower the fire and keep stirring until the scrambled eggs are fluffy and creamy.

4 Add the scrambled egg, avocado, cherry tomatoes and sour cream to the middle of the wraps.

5 Flavour to taste with cayenne pepper and squeeze a drizzle of lime juice on the avocado.

6 Sprinkle the herbs over the top. Fold the bottom of the wrap up and over the filling and roll tightly.

You can make pizzas with leftover wraps. You can also cut the wraps into triangles and fry them up to make crunchy tortilla chips; absolutely yummy with an avocado dip!

Campfire hangover breakfast

» **FIRE** » **PREPARATION IS LESS THAN ½ HOUR** » **SERVES 4** » **BREAKFAST**

INGREDIENTS
+ 6 eggs
+ 500 ml (16 fl oz / 2 cups) milk
+ 1 tbsp (15 g / ½ oz) mustard
+ 100 g (3½ oz / ½ cup) grated cheese
+ 400 g (14 oz / 1 ¾ cups) chorizo, diced
+ oil or full-cream butter
+ salt and pepper
+ 4 thick slices white bread, broken into crumbs
+ 2 spring onions (scallions), cut into fine rings (optional)

We are no strangers to waking up with a hangover after a cosy night by the campfire with new holiday friends and bottles of (cheap) wine. This incredibly scrumptious breakfast and a big cup of coffee are all you need to overcome your campfire hangover. We make this dish in a Dutch oven, but you can also use a cast-iron camp oven.

METHOD

1 Make a fire and wait until it's nearly burned out and the wood smoulders.

2 In a bowl, beat the eggs with the milk and mustard. Stir in cheese and chorizo and add salt and pepper to taste.

3 Grease the Dutch oven with oil or butter.

4 Cover the bottom with breadcrumbs and pour the egg mixture over the top. Cover with a lid.

5 Place the Dutch oven in the fire and add some smouldering pieces of wood on the lid with a pair of tongs. Leave it to cook for approximately 15 to 20 minutes.

6 Serve with spring onions (scallions), extra bread and butter.

Campfire French toast

WITHOUT FLIPPING

» **FIRE** » **PREPARATION IS LONGER THAN ½ HOUR** » **SERVES 4** » **BREAKFAST**

INGREDIENTS
+ ½ loaf of white bread
+ 4 fresh eggs
+ 200 ml (7 fl oz / 1 cup) milk
+ 1 tbsp (15 g / ½ oz) cinnamon
+ pinch of salt

+ punnet (250 g / 1 cup) of strawberries, sliced
+ 1 tbsp (15 g / ½ oz) chopped almonds
+ icing sugar (powdered sugar)
+ maple syrup

The advantage of French toast: you don't have to supervise while you're cooking, the campfire does the hard work for you. So you can just huddle up by the fire with a cup of coffee and patiently wait.

METHOD

1 Make a good fire and put a grill on top.

2 Slice the bread loaf into thick 1 cm (½ inch) slices.

3 Wrap the bottom and half of the loaf in aluminium foil in the shape of a bowl. Make sure nothing can leak from the bottom and the sides.

4 Beat the eggs, milk, cinnamon and salt, and pour the mixture over the entire loaf so it's evenly covered.

5 Add half of the strawberries and almonds between the slices of bread. Keep the rest for garnishing.

6 Place the loaf above the fire for approximately 40 minutes (make sure the fire isn't too hot, the wood should be glowing at this point). The bread is ready when it has absorbed all of the moisture.

7 Remove bread from the fire. Add the remainder of the strawberries and almonds, and top with maple syrup and icing sugar (powdered sugar).

Strawberries taste
best when you
pick them yourself
but buying them is
perfectly fine too.

Always take the scenic route

It's wonderfully relaxing when you don't have to rush for lunch but instead have the luxury of picking the most beautiful spot and taking your time. A glass of wine for the co-driver. Perhaps a little nap in the shade. Mmm ... perhaps we'll just stay here for the night!

a lazy SUMMER AFTERNOON

Rocking the panini

» BARBECUE » PREPARATION IS LESS THAN ½ HOUR » SERVES 4 » LUNCH

INGREDIENTS

+ 1 ciabatta or baguette
+ olive oil
+ 1 tomato, in slices
+ 1 capsicum (pepper), sliced in rings
+ 1 red onion, sliced in rings

+ salami or other cold meats
+ pitted black olives, in slices
+ chunk of cheese of your choice
  (mozzarella, blue, brie or gouda)

While road tripping through Italy we learned that panini is the plural of panino which translates to 'little bread'. Because a sandwich grill was nowhere to be seen during the trip, we came up with the idea to press the bread flat with a big rock; it's a great technique to get that flat panini with perfect grill marks. Below is an example of what you could use, but anything is possible!

METHOD

1 Make sure the barbecue is warm.

2 Cut the bread into four equal parts and halve each part. Grease the outer sides of the bread with a bit of olive oil.

3 Add remaining ingredients to the bottom halves and cover with the top halves of the bread.

4 Place the panini on the barbecue grill and press flat with a big rock (make sure the rock is nice and clean – nobody wants sand between their teeth). Grill the bread until grill marks appear on both sides. The inside should be hot and the cheese melted. This should take approximately 10 minutes depending on the temperature of the barbecue.

✳ Are the panini grilling too fast and starting to burn? Wrap them in aluminium foil and heat them up this way.

TIP:
*No barbecue? You can also grill
the panini in a frying pan on a
camping stove. Flatten with a
rock of course.*

Chicken mayonnaise

GOOD ON A SANDWICH

» **FIRE** » **PREPARATION IS LONGER THAN ½ HOUR** » **SERVES 4** » **LUNCH**

INGREDIENTS

+ 400 g (14 oz / 1½ cups) leftover barbecue chicken or chicken breast
+ 4 tbsp (60 ml / 2 oz) mayonnaise
+ 1 tbsp (15 ml / ½ oz) mustard
+ 1 spring onion (scallion) finely sliced
+ pinch of cayenne pepper
+ handful of finely-chopped flat parsley
+ salt and pepper
+ lime juice
+ 4 lettuce leaves
+ fresh baguette, in 4 pieces, halved
+ chopped red chilli, to taste

You can't toss out leftover roast chicken. You can use it to make delicious chicken mayonnaise sandwich the next day. It's as simple as removing the tender meat, adding mayonnaise and flavour to taste. Slice some bread, add some lettuce leaves, distribute the chicken and you're ready to go.

METHOD

1 If you're using leftover chicken, go to step 2. Otherwise, bring water near boiling point in a big pot. Add the chicken breast (make sure the water doesn't boil). Poach the chicken for five to seven minutes (depending on its size), turn off the fire and drain the water, and leave to cool down inside the pot.

2 Break up the chicken and stir it together with the mayonnaise, mustard, spring onion (scallion), cayenne pepper and parsley. Flavour with salt and pepper and add lime juice (according to taste).

3 Top the sandwich with lettuce and add the chicken mayonnaise mixture. Add the red chilli on top of the mayo.

Top lunch for sure!

Apple pie on the road

» **CAR ENGINE** » **PREPARATION IS OVER 1 HOUR** » **SERVES 4** » **LUNCH**

INGREDIENTS
+ 2 apples, peeled and with core generously removed so they can be stuffed
+ 1 tbsp (13 g / ½ oz) brown sugar
+ 1 tsp (5 g / ⅛ oz) ground cinnamon
+ 1 tbsp (15 g / ½ oz) flaked almonds
+ 1 tbsp (15 g / ½ oz) raisins
+ 2 tbsp (30 g / 1 oz) butter

EQUIPMENT
+ aluminium foil

Feel like warm apple pie but don't have an oven? You can still have it just by keeping your engine running. If you leave at the crack of dawn for your next destination, this 'apple pie' will be ready when you pull over for your first coffee break. Prepare the apple the night before so you don't have to get up early.

METHOD

1 Place each apple on a big piece of aluminium foil.

2 Mix together sugar, cinnamon, flaked almonds and raisins and stuff the apples with it. Make sure you cut a hole big enough in the apple so they can be properly filled. The mixture may overflow a bit, but that's okay.

3 Place a knob of butter on each apple and fold the aluminium parcels tightly to seal. You can also place the apples in a low tin (see Caprese under the hood, p. 59). Make sure no moisture can escape.

4 Place the apples on the warmest part of the engine block and hit the road. After an hour of driving the apples will be soft and warm – a great treat to have with your coffee!

TIP:

For an even greater apple pie experience, you can add cookie crumbs or cake as a crust to the bottom of the parcel. A dollop of whipped cream completes this feast!

Leave the road,
take the trails.

- 45 -

Strong cuppa

COFFEE WITH A BITE!

» FIRE » PREPARATION IS LONGER THAN ½ HOUR » SERVES 2 » AFTERNOON

There's nothing like a good cup of coffee after a long hike or a long journey. You'll definitely regain your energy with this cup of coffee!

Coffee with whiskey

INGREDIENTS
+ 1 tbsp (13 g / ½ oz) instant coffee
+ 2 tbsp (28 g / 1 oz) cacao powder
+ 2 tsp (8 g / ¼ oz) sugar
+ 2 shots (30 ml / 1 fl oz) whiskey
+ boiling water

METHOD

1 Divide the ingredients into two mugs and stir into a paste. Pour boiling water into the mix and give it a good stir.

2 Optional: top with unsweetened whipped cream.

Bitter coffee

INGREDIENTS
+ 2 shots (30 ml / 1 fl oz) espresso
+ Ice cubes if you have them handy
+ 200 ml (7 fl oz / 1 cup) ice-cold tonic water
+ 2 slices of lemon or a wedge of grapefruit

METHOD

1 Prepare the espresso and leave to cool down completely.

2 Divide the ice cubes over two glasses and pour the tonic water over top. Then pour the cold espresso over top.

3 Garnish the drink with a slice of lemon or a wedge of grapefruit.

✱ Make the espresso before you leave. This way it will be nicely cooled down by the time you return from your walk.

Braised cannellini beans

WITH PANCETTA AND ROSEMARY

» FIRE » PREPARATION IS LESS THAN ½ HOUR » SERVES 1 » LUNCH

INGREDIENTS
+ olive oil
+ 2 cloves of garlic, crushed
+ 2 sprigs of fresh rosemary
+ 1 can of cannellini beans, approximately 400 g (14 oz / 1¾ cups)
+ salt and pepper

+ 1 tbsp (15 ml / ½ fl oz) red wine vinegar
+ 4 slices of pancetta

OPTIONAL EQUIPMENT
+ rock for cooking

The Italian cannellini bean is the king of beans. Deliciously full and creamy, and extremely versatile. Serve these braised beans with bread. They make a great standalone lunch meal, a good party snack or a hearty side for a big barbecue. Combined with garlic, rosemary and crispy fried pancetta (cooked on a rock), it is simply divine. You'll be guaranteed to make new road-trip friends with this meal.

METHOD

1 Make a fire and place the grill above it so you can place a pan on it.

2 Add a big splash of olive oil to a cast-iron pan and heat up. Add the garlic and rosemary. Make sure the oil doesn't get too hot and start to bubble. The olive oil should slowly absorb the rich flavours of the garlic and rosemary.

3 Stir in the beans and leave to simmer for 15 minutes. Stir occasionally.

4 Use the rocks heated in the fire to fry the pancetta on. (Of course, you can also just use a frying pan but using a rock is more fun.)

5 Remove beans from the fire and mash with a fork to form a thick puree. Season with salt and pepper, and add some drops of red wine vinegar. Evenly distribute the pancetta in the mashed beans and serve with bread, which you can lightly toast above the fire.

Toast roll-ups

WITH PEAR, FIG AND BLUE CHEESE

» BARBECUE » PREPARATION IS LESS THAN ½ HOUR » SERVES 4 » LUNCH

INGREDIENTS
+ 8 slices of white bread
+ 4 tbsp (86 ml / 2¾ oz) fig jam
+ 1 ripe pear, sliced wafer-thin
+ 100 g (3½ oz / 1 cup) blue cheese, preferably locally made

+ pinch of cayenne pepper
+ handful of chopped walnuts
+ 4 slices of ham
+ olive oil

This is a great dish for lunch, but we prefer to have these toast roll-ups for an evening meal with a nice soup.

METHOD

1 Light the barbecue.

2 Remove the outer crust of the bread and flatten the slices with an empty wine bottle.

3 Use half of the fig jam to spread on the toast. Cover with a thin layer of pear and crumble the cheese in the middle. Sprinkle with a bit of cayenne pepper for extra punch.

4 Scatter the walnuts on the cheese.

5 Roll each slice of bread tightly and wrap each roll with a slice of ham.

6 When the barbecue is at the right temperature, put the rolls on a grill. Grill the rolls for approximately three minutes and turn over regularly so all sides are evenly golden brown.

7 Stir the remaining fig jam with a tablespoon of oil. Remove the rolls from the fire and glaze them with the fig oil. Barbecue for about four minutes until the cheese is melted.

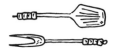

Salad in a jar

INGREDIENTS FOR THE DRESSING
+ 200 ml (7 fl oz / 1 cup) vinegar (great if you can find one that's locally made)
+ 600 ml (20 fl oz / 2½ cups) light olive oil or sunflower seed oil
+ 2 tbsp (40 ml / 1¼ oz) mustard
+ 2 tbsp (43 ml / 1½ oz) honey
+ salt and pepper

OPTIONAL
+ seasoning like cayenne or baharat
+ chopped spring onions (scallions)

INGREDIENTS FOR THE SALAD
Use all your leftovers, and supplement with fresh ingredients if needed. We like to use:
+ leftover barbecue chicken or fish, in small pieces
+ leftover cooked rice or pasta
+ fruit that needs to be used
+ leftover baked potato
+ shredded carrot or even dandelion greens from the roadside
+ leftover cheese
+ nuts and seeds
+ opened tins of beans or corn
+ leftover fresh herbs

Keep glass jars and lids when you're on the road. These come in handy for storing loose tent pole elastics or other items. They keep nuts or salty snacks fresh. They can be used as a salad dressing shaker or to store a salad when on the go – drizzle the salad with a nice dressing and it's perfect. This is a salad dressing recipe with just a suggestion of the types of ingredients you can use to make a great salad. Make the dressing in bulk and store in a jar so it will last for the duration of your road trip. Now you can have lunch with all the leftovers ready in five minutes. Whenever you're making a vinaigrette salad dressing, follow a 3:1 oil to vinegar ratio – three parts oil to one part vinegar. You can't go wrong! If you want more acidity, add more vinegar. If you want more body, add more olive oil.

METHOD

1 Combine salad dressing ingredients in a glass jar and shake vigorously until emulsified. You can also pour the dressing into a clean glass bottle – this will make it easier to use. The oil and vinegar separate into layers after a while. This is completely normal, just shake before use.

Lunch salad

NO-CAMP-STOVE SALAD

» **PREPARATION IS LESS THAN ½ HOUR** » **SERVES 2** » **LUNCH**

INGREDIENTS

+ 200 g (8 oz / 1 cup) baby spinach
+ 100 g (3½ oz / ½ cup) small tomatoes, halved
+ 1 red onion, sliced in rings
+ 1 avocado, sliced
+ 1 mango, sliced
+ 2 tbsp (30 ml / 1 fl oz) dressing (see p. 52)

+ 4 slices of serrano ham
+ 20 g (½ oz / ⅛ cup) pistachios, chopped
+ 50 g (1¾ oz / ¼ cup) goat's cheese, crumbled
+ salt and pepper
+ 1 loaf of bread from the local bakery

Sometimes you end up in a spot where you can't make a fire.
No fire pit, no worries. This meal will save the day. Stop by a local
bakery while on the road. We usually buy a small loaf to take with us
until we can make fresh bread – good as a snack or if you set up camp
in a remote spot where there aren't many shops or the shops have
already closed for the day. If you can't finish the bread, make toast,
French toast (see p. 34) or garlic toast skewers (see p. 126).

METHOD

1 Put the spinach in a big bowl or plate.
Top with tomatoes, onion, avocado and mango.

2 Drizzle with dressing and finish with ham, nuts and goat's cheese.
Season with salt and pepper.

Sardines escabeche

INGREDIENTS

+ 16 farm-fresh whole sardines (not too small)
+ 1 tbsp (18 g / ¾ oz) coarse sea salt
+ small bowl of flour
+ 6 cloves of garlic, thinly sliced
+ olive oil
+ 2 white onions, sliced into small rings
+ 2 glasses of good quality white wine
+ 6 tbsp (90 ml / 3 fl oz) white wine vinegar

+ 1 red chilli pepper, de-seeded, sliced into rings
+ 4 bay leaves
+ 1 tbsp (15 g / ½ oz) capers, rinsed and drained
+ 1 lemon
+ handful of chopped flat-leaf parsley

You can make this dish if you've set up camp by the ocean. You'll need a fridge (or a cool box, esky or cooler) as it's preferable to marinate the sardines for 24 hours. That's when they're at their best. You can also use trout or fresh herring if you can't find fresh sardines.

METHOD

1 Start by cleaning the small fish. Scrub them and remove the insides. Keep the heads on. Rinse them and pat dry. Place the clean sardines on a plate, sprinkle with salt and leave for 30 minutes.

2 Remove the salt and dip the sardines in the bowl of flour.

3 Grill the sardines on the barbecue on both sides for approximately two minutes.

4 To prepare the marinade, fry the sliced garlic and onion rings for about one minute until soft (you could add extra oil in a frying pan). Add red chilli pepper, white wine and vinegar, and simmer for 10 minutes.

5 Place bay leaves and capers on top or between the sardines. Pour the marinade on top and leave to cool down. Refrigerate and allow the flavours to absorb for at least 24 hours.

6 Serve chilled and garnish with slices of lemon and chopped parsley.

It's preferable to marinate the sardines in the fridge but if you don't have one, just marinate the sardines 30 minutes before cooking.

Caprese under the hood

» **CAR ENGINE** » **PREPARATION IS OVER 1 HOUR** » **SERVES 2** » **SIDE DISH**

INGREDIENTS
+ olive oil
+ 1 tbsp (7 g / ⅛ oz) breadcrumbs
+ 2 tomatoes, sliced
+ 1 large ball of mozzarella, in slices
+ 1 red onion, sliced into rings
+ salt and pepper
+ fresh basil
+ balsamic vinegar (optional)

EQUIPMENT
+ clean empty tins
+ aluminium foil

All you have to do for this dish is combine all ingredients in a tin and keep your engine running. Your lunch will be automatically prepared while you're on the road. Isn't that handy?

METHOD

1 Grease the tins and add the breadcrumbs.

2 Cover the bottom with a slice of mozzarella, then add a slice of tomato, a basil leaf and red onion. Repeat the layering until the tin is full. Season each slice of tomato with salt and pepper.

3 Tightly wrap the tins with aluminium foil so they are leak-proof.

4 Place the tin parcels on the warmest part of the engine block and go for a drive. After an hour's drive, the parcels will be warm and the cheese melted. Drizzle with balsamic vinegar. Be careful not to burn your hands when removing the tins from the engine.

✱ See p. 7 for more about cooking on a car engine.

Let's travel the world together

TIME TO GRILL

Road tripping is freedom and adventure. Driving and seeing where you'll end up. Camping where it's pleasant. Making friends on the way. Sitting around the barbecue for a delicious meal.

Quick pasta
WITH ANCHOVIES AND OLIVES

» FIRE » PREPARATION IS LESS THAN ½ HOUR » SERVES 2 » DINNER

INGREDIENTS
+ 300 g (10½ oz / 4 cups) pasta
+ 1 can of anchovies, finely cut
+ 2 cloves of garlic
+ olive oil
+ 2 onions, minced
+ 4 ripe tomatoes, chopped
+ ½ glass of red wine

+ handful of pitted black olives, sliced
+ 1 tbsp (15 g / ½ oz) capers, rinsed and drained
+ chopped oregano
+ salt and pepper
+ fresh basil leaves

This pasta is the perfect dinner after a long hike.

METHOD

1 Cook the pasta al dente according to the packet instructions. Drain the water and keep the pot of pasta covered in a sleeping bag.

2 Crush the garlic and the anchovies into a paste with a rock (or mince these ingredients).

3 Lightly fry the onion with olive oil until translucent and add the garlic mixture. Fry on a low fire and stir constantly until the anchovies begin to melt into the oil.

4 Add the tomatoes and red wine, and simmer on a low fire until you get a beautiful sauce.

5 Add olives, capers and oregano, and season the sauce with salt and pepper. Tear the basil and stir into the sauce when almost finished.

6 Mix the pasta with the warm sauce and serve.

❋ You can also have the sauce with bread if you don't have pasta or if you only have one pot to cook with. You can also use the sauce to make nacho pizza (see p. 155).

CHAPTER 3: EVENING »

- 62 -

TIP:
*You could use the roasted garlic
(see p. 99) if you've made this in
advance. It will be even tastier and
the meal will be cooked even faster!*

see p. 99

*If you don't have
sea lavender or
pickleweed you can use
baby spinach instead.*

Cockles from the sand

WITH PASTA AND PICKLEWEED

» **FIRE** » **PREPARATION IS LONGER THAN ½ HOUR** » **SERVES 4** » **DINNER**

INGREDIENTS
+ 300 g (10½ oz / 4 cups) spaghetti
+ olive oil
+ 2 cloves of garlic, finely minced
+ 1 shallot, minced
+ ½ red chilli pepper, cleaned, finely diced
+ 1 large glass of white wine

+ 1 kg (2.2 lb) fresh cockles, well rinsed
+ 200 g (7 oz / 1 cup) tomatoes, diced
+ bunch of parsley, chopped
+ 50 g (1¾ oz / ¼ cup) sea lavender
+ handful of pickleweed, washed
+ salt and pepper

We would often go to Bretagne in France when we were young. When the tide was low, we would collect cockles with our little buckets and spades, just like the locals. It was so much fun! And then we would get together as a family and cook them.

METHOD

1 Cook the pasta al dente, drain the water and keep the pot of pasta covered in a sleeping bag.

2 Heat 2 tbsp (27 ml) of oil in a large frying pan and fry the garlic, shallot and red chilli pepper. Add the white wine to the pan.

3 Bring the wine to the boil and add the cockles and tomatoes. Toss occasionally.

4 Add parsley (leave some for garnish), pickleweed and sea lavender when almost finished. The cockles are ready when they are completely open. Season the sauce with salt and pepper but don't overdo it with the salt.

5 Mix the pasta in with the sauce and garnish with parsley. Serve with a piece of bread for dipping and a large glass of chilled white wine.

Tempeh satay

WITH COCONUT MILK AND RED CHILLI

» **BARBECUE** » **PREPARATION IS OVER 1 HOUR** » **SERVES 2** » **DINNER**

INGREDIENTS
+ 250 g (1¾ oz / ¼ cup) tempeh
+ 145 ml (5 fl oz / ½ cup) sweet soy sauce (kecap manis)
+ 1 tbsp (13 ml / ½ fl oz) sunflower oil
+ 1 tbsp (15 ml / ½ fl oz) sambal
+ juice of 1 lime
+ 1 tbsp (15 g / ½ oz) five-spice powder
+ 2 cloves of garlic, minced
+ 2 tbsp (32 g / 1 oz) peanut butter
+ 200 ml (7 fl oz / 1 cup) coconut milk

+ 1 red chilli pepper, de-seeded and finely chopped
+ salt and pepper
+ 2 spring onions (scallions), sliced in rings
+ 1 tbsp (5 g / ⅛ oz) chopped coriander (cilantro)
+ 1 tbsp (4 g / ⅛ oz) toasted sesame seeds (optional)

EQUIPMENT
+ skewers

Marinate the tempeh for optimum taste. If you do this in the morning and place the tempeh in the esky (cool box or cooler) and go about your day, you'll have a super-quick and delicious meal in the evening.

METHOD

1 Cut the tempeh into 1 cm (½ inch) cubes. Make a marinade with half of the sweet soy sauce, the sunflower oil, sambal, lime juice, five-spice powder and one clove of garlic. Add the tempeh and marinate for at least two hours. The longer the tastier.

2 Light the barbecue.

3 Make the sauce. Add the peanut butter, the remaining sweet soy sauce, coconut milk, red chilli pepper and the remaining garlic in a little frying pan and stir into a smooth sauce. Season with salt and pepper.

4 Thread the tempeh pieces onto the skewers and grill on the barbecue on all sides until cooked and golden brown.

5 Serve with the sauce and garnish with spring onions (scallions), coriander (cilantro) and sesame seeds.

❋ Delicious with a super-quick Indonesian potato salad (see p. 125).

TIP:
You can pre-prepare the dry rubs at home and take them on your travels in well-sealed tins or containers.

Rub it in

When you take these pre-prepared homemade rubs in pots on your road trip, you can add instant flavour to a good cut of meat, fish or grilled vegetables for dinner. You really don't need much else.

Spicy coffee rub

For approximately 500 g (17 oz) of beef like ribeye or flank steak
+ 4 tbsp (56 g / 2 oz) coffee, finely ground
+ 2 tsp (8 g / ¼ oz) chipotle, ground
+ 2 tsp (8 g / ¼ oz) brown sugar
+ 2 tbsp (25 g / 1 oz) smoked paprika powder
+ salt and pepper

Combine all ingredients and mix thoroughly. Rub the meat with the dry mixture and allow to sit for 45 to 60 minutes. Slow-grill the meat on the barbecue on indirect fire until it is cooked to your liking.

Curry–orange rub

For 500 g (17 oz) of chicken (thigh or drumstick)
+ dried zest of 1 orange (dry for a couple of hours on a tea towel in the sun)
+ 1 tbsp (13 g / ½ oz) curry powder
+ 1 tsp (8 g / ¼ oz) coriander (cilantro) seeds, crushed
+ 1 tsp (5 g / ⅛ oz) ginger powder
+ 1 tbsp (13 g / ½ oz) white sugar

Combine all ingredients and mix very well. Rub the chicken with the dry mixture and allow to sit for 30 minutes. Roast the chicken on the barbecue or at a low temperature. Chicken tends to dry out, but if you control the temperature carefully this won't happen.

Fennel–lemon-dill rub

For 500 g (17 oz) fish
+ 1 tbsp (8 g / ¼ oz) fennel seeds, crushed
+ 1 tsp (5 g / ⅛ oz) dried dill
+ Dried zest of 1 lemon (dry for a couple of hours on a cloth out in the sun)
+ 1 tsp (4 g / ⅛ oz) white sugar
+ freshly ground black pepper and salt

Combine all ingredients and mix very well. Rub the fish with the mixture before grilling.

S'mores

WITH MARSHMALLOWS AND STRAWBERRIES

» **FIRE** » **PREPARATION IS LESS THAN ½ HOUR** » **SERVES 4** » **DESSERT**

INGREDIENTS
+ 1 big bag of marshmallows
+ 1 packet of plain, sweet biscuits
+ 1 large bar of chocolate, grated
+ 1 punnet (250 g / 1 cup) strawberries (or raspberries), sliced
+ 1 jar of peanut butter
+ 1 banana, thinly sliced
+ fudge, in small pieces

EQUIPMENT
+ aluminium foil
+ long twigs / skewers

I would have sworn that the word s'more is originally Scandinavian. It sounds incredibly Swedish, right? While making this book I discovered that the s'more is American and comes from 'some more' which is, of course, difficult to pronounce with a mouth full of sticky sweetness. We thought up some different versions of s'mores that are even better than the original.

METHOD

1 Make a campfire

2 Lay the biscuits out on a piece of aluminium foil and add a generous amount of chocolate to each one. Top with fruit, peanut butter and fudge.

3 Thread the marshmallows on a stick and hold them over the fire. They're ready when they puff up and turn light brown.

4 Use a biscuit to slide the cooked marshmallow onto another biscuit. Gently squeeze the marshmallow down and sandwich together with one of the prepared biscuits. The hot marshmallows will melt the other ingredients, which tastes divine.

✱ Use leftover wraps (see p. 30) instead of biscuits. Place all the ingredients over one wrap and place a second one on top.

America meets Mexico!

It will be a sticky affair.
Keep a wet cloth on hand
to keep your fingers clean.

Couscous salad

WITH PRUNES AND GOAT'S CHEESE

» **FIRE** » **PREPARATION IS LESS THAN ½ HOUR** » **SERVES 4** » **DINNER**

INGREDIENTS

+ 400 ml (2 cups) water or vegetable stock
+ 250 g (6 oz / 1⅓ cups) couscous
+ 2 tbsp (30 g / 1 oz) raisins
+ 5 dried prunes, cut into pieces
+ 1 shallot, finely diced
+ 200 g (7 oz / 2 cups) small tomatoes, halved
+ 1 cucumber, de-seeded, cut into cubes

+ 2 tbsp (30 g / 1 oz) chopped mint
+ 1 tbsp (15 g / ½ oz) cinnamon
+ ½ tbsp (4 g / ⅛ oz) cayenne pepper
+ olive oil
+ lemon juice
+ salt and pepper
+ 150 g (5½ oz / 1 cup) soft goat's cheese

This recipe is one of our road trip favourites. You pour some boiling water over the couscous and then all you do is wait a little. It's particularly quick when you use ingredients that don't require a lot of cutting and chopping. Use up what's leftover and use local produce to create your favourite taste combinations.

METHOD

1 Bring the water to the boil (or use vegetable stock for an even tastier option).

2 Add the couscous, raisins and prunes into a pot and pour the boiling water over top. Close the lid and leave to stand for approximately eight minutes or until the liquid has been absorbed.

3 Fluff the couscous with a fork and let it cool down. Add the remaining ingredients. Add a drizzle of olive oil and lemon juice. Combine well and season with salt and pepper.

4 Crumble the cheese on top and serve.

✱ Tasty with a yoghurt dip and fresh bread.

Grilled eggplants (aubergines)
WITH MINT AND BASIL

» **BARBECUE** » **PREPARATION IS LESS THAN ½ HOUR** » **SERVES 2** » **DINNER**

INGREDIENTS
+ 2 eggplants (aubergines), thinly sliced
+ salt and pepper
+ 2 cloves of garlic, minced
+ olive oil

+ red wine vinegar
+ 1 tbsp (15 g / ½ oz) chopped mint
+ 1 tbsp (15 g / ½ oz) chopped basil
+ 1 tbsp (15 g / ½ oz) toasted pine nuts

Make a lot of these! The eggplant (aubergine) is even better chilled the next day to pack for lunch on the road.

METHOD

1 Light the barbecue.

2 Sprinkle the slices of eggplant (aubergine) with salt and allow to sit until the moisture is extracted. Then pat dry with a paper towel.

3 Combine the garlic, oil and some pepper and cover the eggplant (aubergine) slices with the mixture.

4 Grill both sides of the eggplant (aubergine) on the barbecue until cooked. Place on a plate, drizzle with a dash of red wine vinegar and sprinkle with mint, basil and pine nuts.

Warm salad
PUFFED BEET, RADISH AND SAUSAGE

» **BARBECUE / FIRE** » **PREPARATION IS OVER 1 HOUR** » **SERVES 2** » **DINNER**

INGREDIENTS
+ 4 raw beetroots, peeled
+ olive oil
+ salt and pepper
+ 4 sprigs of thyme
+ 1 bunch of radishes, washed and without leaves
+ 1 tbsp (15 ml / ½ fl oz) balsamic vinegar
+ ¾ tbsp (11 ml / ¼ oz) ginger syrup (or honey)

+ 4 bratwurst (or pork or veal) sausages
+ 100 g (3½ oz / 3⅓ cups) rocket (arugula)
+ 1 apple, peeled and in wedges
+ 1 red onion, in wedges
+ 2 tbsp (30 g / 1 oz) chopped chives
+ Handful of chopped pecans

EQUIPMENT
+ aluminium foil

METHOD

1 Light the barbecue or make a fire.

2 Place each beetroot on a piece of aluminium foil and drizzle with oil. Sprinkle with salt and pepper and add a sprig of thyme. Wrap the beetroots well and place on the barbecue for approximately one hour until cooked (check by pricking with a cocktail pick or knife). Leave to cool down until you can unwrap the beetroot.

3 Put the radishes together in a piece of aluminium foil, drizzle with oil and sprinkle with salt. Tightly wrap the foil and place with the beetroot parcels on the fire for the final 20 minutes of cooking.

4 Make a dressing of three tbsp of olive oil, balsamic vinegar, ginger syrup and salt and pepper.

5 Grill the sausages on the barbecue until they are nicely brown and cooked. Cut into slices.

6 Cut the roasted beetroots in wedges and halve the radishes. Combine in a bowl with rocket, apple and red onion. Drizzle with the dressing and top with chives and chopped nuts. Scatter the sausage slices over the salad and serve warm with bread.

Asian-style cockles

WITH CORIANDER (CILANTRO) AND COCONUT MILK

» **BARBECUE** » **PREPARATION IS LESS THAN ½ HOUR** » **SERVES 4** » **DINNER**

INGREDIENTS
+ 2 kg (4½ lbs) mussels or other shellfish
+ 1 generous knob of butter
+ 2 shallots, minced
+ 2 cloves of garlic, finely chopped
+ 1 red chilli pepper, cut into small rings
+ 2 stalks of lemongrass, sliced in half lengthways

+ 200 ml (7 fl oz / 1 cup) coconut milk
+ salt and pepper
+ handful of chopped coriander (cilantro)
+ juice of 1 lime

You're not always allowed to use a barbecue in places where you camp overnight. No worries, you can often use a public barbecue if one is available. This is great as people are often attracted by the delicious aroma and hang around for a chat.

METHOD

1 Light the barbecue and wait until the coals are glowing.

2 Wash the cockles well and leave to drain. Discard broken and/or open cockles.

3 Add the butter to a deep roasting tray or deep oven tray and allow to heat on the barbecue. Lightly fry the shallots, garlic, red chilli peppers and lemongrass for about a minute and add the shellfish. Stir the ingredients well and add the coconut milk. The cockles are done as soon as they are all opened.

4 Season with salt, pepper and coriander (cilantro), and drizzle with lime juice.

✱ Tasty with the cucumber salad (see p. 91) and some fresh crispy bread.

Escape and breathe the air of new places.

- 80 -

- 81 -

Grilled green romano beans
WITH GARLIC, FETA AND TARRAGON

» BARBECUE » PREPARATION IS LONGER THAN ½ HOUR » SERVES 4 » DINNER

INGREDIENTS
+ 3 tbsp (40 ml / 1¼ fl oz) olive oil
+ juice of ½ a lemon
+ 2 tbsp (30 g / 1 oz) chopped tarragon (fresh)
+ 1 clove of garlic, pressed or pestled with a rock
+ salt and pepper
+ big pot of romano beans (or snap or broad beans)
+ thick slice of feta cheese

These romano beans are delightful, especially when they are fresh off the barbecue. The tarragon's liquorice flavours combine very well with the sweetness of the beans and the savoury flavour of the feta. We eat them on the go, often as a snack, but they are also great as a side with a grilled piece of meat and a baked potato.

METHOD

1 Make sure the barbecue is warm.

2 Stir oil, lemon juice, tarragon (leave some for garnish), garlic, and salt and pepper together well and pour over the romano beans. Give it a good shake so all beans are nicely coated with the oil.

3 Place the beans on the barbecue grill and turn them over after about four minutes. Remove from the barbecue after eight minutes (it's okay if they turn a bit brown) and allow to sit for five minutes.

4 Crumble the feta on the beans and drizzle with a bit of oil. Garnish with the remaining tarragon.

✱ Substitute the crumbled feta with a hard boiled egg and black olives.

- 83 -

Easy peasy sauces and dips

Sauces and dips go well with just about anything you eat. Below are a number of recipes for simple sauces and dips with a base of mayonnaise, yoghurt or olive oil.

Mayonnaise-based dip (4 tbsp / 60 ml / 2 fl oz)

+ 2 tbsp (30 ml / 1 oz) mustard and 1 tsp of honey (7 g / ⅛ oz)
+ Or with 1 tsp (5 g / ⅛ oz) wasabi, 1 tbsp (15 g / ½ oz) chopped coriander (cilantro) and 1 tbsp (15 ml / ½ fl oz) soy sauce
+ Or with 2 tbsp (30 g / 1 oz) finely-diced fresh herbs and 1 tbsp (15 g / ½ oz) minced onion
+ Or with 2 cloves of finely-diced garlic, 1 tbsp (13 ml / ½ fl oz) olive oil and a pinch of cinnamon
+ Or with 1 tbsp (15 g / ½ oz) each finely diced chives, chopped onion and chopped chives, and 1 finely-diced hard-boiled egg

Combine all ingredients and season with salt and pepper. This goes well with potatoes, meat or as a spread.

Yoghurt-based dip (4 tbsp / 60 ml / 2 fl oz)

+ ½ cucumber, grated and drained, and 1 pressed clove of garlic
+ Or with 2 tbsp (30 g / 1 oz) mayonnaise and 2 cloves of pressed garlic
+ Or with 2 tbsp (30 g / 1 oz) chopped nuts and 1 tbsp (15ml / ½ oz) finely-chopped sundried tomatoes
+ Or with the pulp of 1 grilled eggplant (aubergine), 1 clove of finely-chopped garlic and 1 tsp (5 g / ⅛ oz) finely-chopped flat-leaf parsley
+ Or with 1 tbsp (15 ml / ½ fl oz) lemon juice, ½ tbsp (7 ml / ¼ oz) mustard and 2 tbsp (30 g / 1 oz) finely-chopped dill

Combine all ingredients. Nice and fresh with a salad, on bread or with a barbecued piece of meat or fish.

Olive oil-based dip
(4 tbsp / 60 ml / 2 fl oz)

+ 2 tsp (14 g / ½ oz) honey, 2 tbsp
  (43 ml / 1½ fl oz) vinegar, 2 tsp
  (30 ml / 1 oz) mustard and 1 tbsp
  (15 g / ½ oz) finely-chopped dill
+ Or with 2 tbsp (30 ml / 1 fl oz) orange
  juice, 1 tbsp (15 g / ½ oz) finely-chopped
  tarragon and 1 tbsp (15 ml / ½ fl oz)
  red wine vinegar
+ Or with 3 tbsp (40 ml / 1¼ fl oz) balsamic
  vinegar, 2 tsp (10 ml / ¼ oz) mustard
  and 1 clove of finely-chopped garlic
+ Or with 1 tsp (4 ml / ⅛ fl oz) sesame oil,
  1 tbsp (15 ml / ½ fl oz) rice wine vinegar,
  1 tbsp (15 ml / ½ fl oz) soy sauce, 1 tsp
  (7 g / ⅛ oz) honey, 1 tsp (5 g / ⅛ oz)
  grated ginger and a pinch of chilli pepper
+ Or with 1 tbsp (15 g / ½ oz) finely-
  chopped anchovies, 2 tbsp (30 ml / 1 fl oz)
  white wine vinegar, 1 tbsp (15 g / ½ oz)
  finely-diced onion and 1 tbsp (15 g / ½ oz)
  finely-chopped flat-leaf parsley

Combine the ingredients in a pot with
salt and pepper. Cover with the lid and
shake until well mixed. This dip is great
with bread or as a salad dressing. Also
good to add flavour to roasted potatoes,
vegetables, or to quickly glaze bread
before toasting it.

Fish from the newspaper

WITH FENNEL, DILL AND LEMON THYME

» **FIRE / BARBECUE** » **PREPARATION IS LONGER THAN ½ HOUR** » **SERVES 2** » **DINNER**

INGREDIENTS
+ 2 fresh trout, cleaned
+ salt and pepper
+ olive oil
+ handful of dill
+ 4 sprigs of lemon thyme
+ ½ fennel bulb, in thin slices

+ 1 lemon, sliced
+ 1 tsp (5 g / ⅛ oz) fennel seeds, crushed

EQUIPMENT
+ newspaper
+ string

Cooking fish above a fire in a wet newspaper is a fantastically unique experience for your tastebuds! The newspaper starts to scorch which creates a wonderfully smoky flavour. You can use all kinds of fish for this recipe but we chose trout. Make sure the newspaper is nice and wet.

METHOD

1 Light a fire or barbecue and wait until it smoulders.

2 Rub the fish with oil, salt and pepper and stuff the fish cavity with half of the spices, fennel and lemon.

3 Place the newspaper open in the centrefold and add some spices and fennel on top. Then add the trout on the bed of spices and fennel, and scatter the remaining spices, fennel and lemon on the fish. Drizzle with olive oil.

4 Roll the fish up tightly in the newspaper and tie with string. Soak the parcel by placing it in a tub of water.

5 Place on a grill over the fire. Depending on the size of the fish and the fire temperature, the fish should cook in approximately 15 minutes.

Hearty lentil soup

« CHAPTER 3: EVENING »

INGREDIENTS
+ splash of oil
+ 1 onion, chopped
+ 1 clove of garlic, crushed
+ 1 small carrot, diced or sliced
+ 2 stalks of celery, peeled and cut into pieces
+ 1 capsicum (pepper), de-seeded and cut into pieces
+ 1 tbsp (15 ml / ½ oz) of a spice mix (eg. baharat or vadouvan)

+ 500 g (17 oz / 2 cups) canned tomatoes, strained
+ 400 g (14 oz / 1½ cups) canned lentils, rinsed
+ 500 ml (16 fl oz / 2 cups) water
+ handful of chopped green herbs, for example flat-leaf parsley, chives or coriander (cilantro)
+ salt and pepper

We are often very hungry after a big hike, but the will to cook is usually nowhere to be found. This lentil soup stands out for its simplicity and will be steaming hot right in front of you in *no time*.

METHOD

1 Make a good fire and wait until it smoulders.

2 Heat the oil in a deep pan. Lightly fry the onion, garlic, carrot, celery and capsicum (pepper) until everything is nice and translucent. Add the spice mix and fry for a minute.

3 Add the strained tomatoes, lentils and water and stir through. Simmer for five minutes

4 Top the soup with chopped herbs and season with salt and pepper. Serve with a hearty slice of bread and full-cream butter.

✻ You can make this vegetarian soup even more hearty by adding meat, for example fried chorizo, bacon or smoked sausage.

Prefer fish? Codfish or another type of hearty white fish goes well too.

Do you have leftover carrots and celery? Use these the next day in a salad, risotto (see p. 103) or chicken stew (see p. 117).

Cucumber salad

WITH FETA, MINT AND DILL

INGREDIENTS
+ 3 tbsp (40 ml / 1¼ fl oz) olive oil
+ 1 tbsp (15 ml / ½ fl oz) lemon juice
+ 1 tsp (7 g / ⅛ oz) honey
+ Salt and pepper
+ 2 cucumbers, de-seeded, sliced

+ 1 red onion, in wedges
+ 1 tbsp (15 g / ½ oz) chopped dill
+ 1 tbsp (15 g / ½ oz) chopped mint
+ 1 tsp (4 g / ⅛ oz) honey or sugar
+ 125 g (4½ oz / ½ cup) feta

Cucumber is great anytime, anywhere – as a snack, as flavour infusion in thirst-quenching water, as an after-sun treatment on sunburnt cheeks, as soothing beauty treatment for tired eyes and above all, as simple greens for quick salads.

METHOD

1 Combine and stir the oil, lemon juice and honey, and season with salt and pepper.

2 Combine the dressing with the cucumber, onion and chopped herbs and crumble feta on top.

3 Serve with fresh bread or baked potatoes.

Barbecue caesar salad

» **BARBECUE** » **PREPARATION IS LONGER THAN ½ HOUR** » **SERVES 4** » **DINNER**

INGREDIENTS FOR THE DRESSING
+ 2 egg yolks
+ 2 cloves of garlic, finely crushed or diced
+ 3 anchovy fillets, chopped
+ 1 tbsp (15 ml / ½ oz) mustard
+ juice and zest of 1 lemon
+ 300 ml (1¼ cups) sunflower oil

INGREDIENTS FOR THE SALAD
+ 4 hard-boiled eggs
+ 1 loaf stale bread (baguette, ciabatta or farmer's bread)
+ 1 clove of garlic, sliced
+ salt
+ olive oil
+ 1 romaine lettuce or 2 baby cos lettuces, washed and drained
+ 50 g (1¾ oz / ¼ cup) grated parmesan cheese

For this salad, wrap the eggs in aluminium foil with a bit of water and a sprig of rosemary, and place amongst the coals for seven minutes. You'll have the perfect hard-boiled eggs. Another golden tip: cook all the eggs in the carton. Hard-boiled eggs keep well for a while and make a great snack on the go.

METHOD

1 Light the barbecue and wait until the coals glow.

2 Make the dressing: add the yolks with the garlic, mustard, anchovies, lemon zest and juice into a bowl and whisk while adding the oil. Keep whisking until you have a thick mayonnaise.

3 Tear the bread into large pieces and place on a cast-iron roasting pan. Add the garlic and lightly sprinkle with salt. Drizzle with olive oil and give a good shake.

4 Place the roasting pan on the coals and toast the croutons until crispy. Turn occasionally until evenly browned.

5 Tear the lettuce into pieces and stir in 4 tbsp of the dressing. Finish the salad by adding the croutons, eggs and parmesan. Serve with a delicious barbecue grilled chicken.

The mayonnaise will be at its best if all ingredients are at room temperature.

Orange and fennel salad

WITH VARIATIONS

» **PREPARATION IS LESS THAN ½ HOUR** » **SERVES 2** » **DINNER**

INGREDIENTS
+ 1 tbsp (15 ml / ½ fl oz) orange juice
+ 1 tbsp (15 ml / ½ fl oz) red wine vinegar
+ 1 tbsp (13 ml / ½ fl oz) olive oil
+ 1 tsp (5 g / ⅛ oz) mustard
+ handful of chopped tarragon or dill
+ salt and pepper
+ 1 fennel bulb, in wafer-thin slices
+ 2 oranges, thinly sliced

OPTIONAL
+ handful of raisins, chopped dried apricots or chopped walnuts
+ juice of ½ a lemon
+ 1 clove of garlic, finely chopped or crushed
+ salt and pepper
+ 250 g (9 oz / 1 cup) sweet vine-ripened cocktail tomatoes, optionally roasted on the barbecue

**This quick salad with fennel and orange is a crowd-pleaser.
It pairs very well with grilled chicken or fish, but also with pasta.**

METHOD

1 Combine the orange juice, vinegar, oil and mustard and season with the chopped herbs, and salt and pepper.

2 Add the fennel and orange slices to a deep plate or bowl and pour the dressing over.

3 Leave the flavours to absorb and top with raisins, chopped apricots and/or walnuts.

Also tasty with red onion and radish.

Grilled baby potatoes
WITH SOUR CREAM AND DILL SAUCE

» **BARBECUE / FIRE** » **PREPARATION IS LESS THAN ½ HOUR** » **SERVES 4** » **DINNER**

INGREDIENTS
+ 16 baby potatoes with skin on
+ 2 shallots, sliced into rings
+ 1 clove of garlic, finely chopped
+ olive oil
+ 12 bay leaves
+ 125 ml (4¼ fl oz / ½ cup) sour cream

+ zest of 1 lime
+ handful of chopped dill
+ coarse sea salt and pepper

EQUIPMENT
+ 8 metal or wooden skewers

We always take metal barbecue skewers with us when we travel, so we can use the skewers everywhere we go. You can also use wooden skewers. To make sure the wooden skewers don't catch fire on the barbecue, soak them in water for about 30 minutes before use.

METHOD

1 Light the barbecue or a fire.

2 Add the baby potatoes to a bowl and mix with the onion, garlic and a splash of oil. Thread and alternate the baby potatoes, onion and bay leaves on the skewers.

3 Roast for approximately six minutes until the potatoes are browned and cooked through. Turn skewers over halfway through.

4 Combine the sour cream, dill and lime zest. Season with salt and pepper.

5 Place the baby potato skewers on a plate and sprinkle with coarse sea salt.

6 Serve with the dill sauce.

Roasted garlic

STRAIGHT OUT OF THE FIRE

» **FIRE / BARBECUE** » **PREPARATION IS OVER 1 HOUR** » **SERVES 1 + EXTRA** » **SIDE**

INGREDIENTS
+ garlic bulbs
+ olive oil
+ salt

EQUIPMENT
+ aluminium foil

You can keep this fire-roasted garlic for a long time by storing the cloves in clean, empty glass jars covered with oil and the lid on. An added bonus is that the oil becomes deliciously garlicky and can be used for everything.

METHOD

1 Make a fire or light the barbecue.

2 Cut the top off each garlic bulb so you can see the cloves.

3 Place each bulb on a piece of aluminium foil, drizzle with olive oil and sprinkle with a bit of salt. Tightly wrap the aluminium foil and place the bulbs in the campfire ashes.

4 Leave to cook in the ashes for about one hour and remove with tongs.

5 Leave to cool down and push the soft cloves out of the bulb into a container. They're now ready for use, as simple as that!

✽ Bake the garlic if you've already got a fire going. Roast a couple of bulbs at the same time. Keep the garlic in an empty jam jar.

Pasta with pesto

EASY FOR ON THE WAY

» FIRE » PREPARATION IS LESS THAN ½ HOUR » SERVES 4 » DINNER

INGREDIENTS
+ 250 g (6 oz / 1⅓ cups) pasta
+ 300 g (10½ oz / 2 cups) peas, blanched
+ 100 g (3½ oz / ½ cup) fresh basil, roughly torn
+ 60 g (2 oz / ½ cup) grated parmesan cheese
+ 1 clove of garlic, finely chopped or crushed
+ drizzle of good olive oil
+ juice of ½ a lemon
+ salt and pepper
+ 50 g (1¾ oz / ¼ cup) pine nuts, toasted
+ 250 g (6 oz / 1⅓ cups) sweet vine-ripened cocktail tomatoes, roasted on the barbecue (optional)

At home we've always got a fresh jar of pesto ready. We use it almost daily as a dip, with pasta or on bread. This pre-made pesto is a great alternative for on the road when you don't have a food processor.

METHOD

1 Cook the pasta al dente according to packet instructions.

2 Stir the parmesan cheese (keep some for later), peas, garlic and basil (keep some aside as well) in with the pasta.

3 Drizzle some oil and lemon juice to taste and season with salt and pepper. Toss the pasta while warm.

4 Divide the pasta into bowls and garnish with the leftover basil and parmesan, and add the toasted pine nuts and cocktail tomatoes. Too easy!

✱ Make an extra quantity; this pasta is also nice when served cold. Great for lunch when you're on the go.

WILD VARIETY
Replace the mushrooms with hand-picked dandelion greens, nettle leaves or ground elder. Chop this very finely and add in the pan with the shallots, garlic and celery.

Road-trip risotto

INGREDIENTS

+ 750 ml (25½ fl oz / 3¼ cups) vegetable or mushroom stock
+ 250 g (6 oz / 1⅓ cups) mushrooms, brushed clean, in pieces
+ leaves of 2 sprigs of thyme
+ leaves of 1 sprig of rosemary
+ olive oil
+ salt and pepper
+ 1 tbsp (15 g / ½ oz) full-cream butter
+ 2 finely-diced shallots
+ 2 cloves of garlic, pressed
+ 2 stalks of celery, peeled and cut into pieces
+ 300 g (10½ oz / 1½ cups) risotto
+ 1 glass of dry white wine
+ 75 g (2¾ oz / ⅔ cup) grated parmesan cheese
+ 50 g (1¾ oz / ¼ cup) full-cream butter to top

Wherever we are, we always dish up a good pot of risotto. Even on the road. Preferably with local ingredients, of course.

METHOD

1 Bring the stock to the boil.

2 Using a pan with a thicker base, fry the mushrooms in a bit of oil until they start to shrink and turn brown. Add thyme and rosemary towards the end and fry with the mushrooms. Season the mixture with salt and pepper, remove from the pan and store for later use.

3 Add a bit of oil with the butter in the same pan and fry the shallots, garlic and celery until translucent. Add the rice and keep stirring, making sure that the rice doesn't brown. Pour the wine in and keep stirring. Lower the fire. Once the wine is absorbed, add the stock a spoonful at a time, stirring continuously. Wait until the rice has absorbed the moisture before adding another spoonful and continue stirring.

4 The rice should be cooked after 15 to 20 minutes. Remove the pot from the fire and stir in the mushrooms, parmesan cheese and full-cream butter. One final important step for making the perfect risotto – keep the lid on the pot for two minutes. This will make it even creamier.

Greek burgers
WITH RADISH TZATZIKI

» BARBECUE » PREPARATION IS LONGER THAN ½ HOUR » SERVES 4 » DINNER

INGREDIENTS FOR THE TZATZIKI
+ 200 ml (7 oz / 1 cup) thick Turkish yoghurt
+ 1 bunch of radishes, very finely chopped or grated
+ 1 clove of garlic, very finely chopped
+ 1 tbsp (15 g / ½ oz) chives, cut into small pieces
+ 1 tbsp (15 g / ½ oz) chopped dill or mint
+ 1 tbsp (13 ml / ½ fl oz) olive oil
+ squeeze of lemon juice for taste
+ salt and pepper

INGREDIENTS FOR THE BURGERS
+ 500 g (17 oz / 2 cups) lamb or beef mince
+ 1 tbsp (15 g / ½ oz) chopped oregano
+ 1 tsp (5 g / ⅛ oz) paprika powder
+ dash of cinnamon
+ 1 shallot, finely diced
+ salt and pepper

We love tzatziki and eat it regularly. It reminds us of our travels to the Greek islands. We came up with this version with radishes when we were left without cucumber one day. A successful experiment! Especially good for a juicy barbecued burger with a Greek twist.

METHOD

1 Light the barbecue.

2 Prepare the tzatziki by mixing all the ingredients.

3 Knead the ingredients for the burger and form four flat patties.

4 Fry the burgers on the barbecue until nicely brown and cooked. We prefer them slightly pink inside. Serve with pita bread toasted on the barbecue.

❋ You can grill and serve some eggplant (aubergine) and zucchini (courgette) slices as a side.

Travel and see the unseen.

Baked potato
WITH SOUR CREAM

» **BARBECUE** » **PREPARATION IS LONGER THAN ½ HOUR** » **SERVES 2** » **DINNER**

INGREDIENTS
+ 2 large potatoes
+ olive oil
+ coarse sea salt
+ knob of full-cream butter
+ 2 tbsp (30 ml / 1 oz) sour cream

+ 1 tbsp (15 g / ½ oz) chopped chives
+ salt and pepper

EQUIPMENT
+ aluminium foil

The humble baked potato is nutritious, tasty and incredibly easy to make. Everybody loves it. Take a bag of potatoes with you if you want to make friends at the campfire. Place them tightly-wrapped in aluminium foil in the campfire ashes or in the corner of the barbecue. You can do your thing while the potatoes bake.

METHOD

1 Scrub the potatoes clean. Puncture holes with a fork. Place each potato on a large piece of aluminium foil, drizzle with olive oil and sprinkle with coarse sea salt.

2 Tightly wrap the foil and place the potatoes at the edge of the fire or on the side of glowing coals on the barbecue so they don't get too hot. Bake for approximately 30 minutes.

3 Remove the potatoes from the fire and leave to cool down so you can grab them with your fingers.

4 Open the parcel, slice the potato lengthwise down the centre and mash the insides with a fork. Stir in some sour cream, chopped chives and full-cream butter and sprinkle with salt and pepper.

✱ Other great fillings are:
+ *brie, spring onions (scallions) and full-cream butter*
+ *fried bacon, diced avocado, finely-diced onion and diced tomato*
+ *smoked strips of salmon, sour cream, black pepper*
+ *leftover bean stew (see p. 48)*
+ *blue cheese, chopped walnuts, dried figs cut in pieces, full-cream butter.*

Slow celeriac

WITH QUICK MUSTARD SAUCE

» BARBECUE » PREPARATION IS OVER 1 HOUR » SERVES 4 » DINNER

INGREDIENTS
+ 1 celeriac bulb (celery root)
+ 4 tbsp (53 ml / 1¾ fl oz) olive oil
+ salt and pepper
+ loose cloves of garlic from one bulb
+ bunch of thyme or sprigs of rosemary
+ black pepper
+ 1 big tbsp (15 ml / ½ oz) mustard

+ 1 big glass of white wine (sauvignon blanc goes well)
+ small cup of whipped cream
+ 1 tbsp (15 ml / ½ oz) chopped tarragon, parsley or dill

EQUIPMENT
+ aluminium foil

METHOD

1 Light the barbecue and wait until the coals glow.

2 Peel the celeriac, wash and dry thoroughly. Rub the celeriac with oil and place in a big piece of double-folded aluminium foil. Sprinkle with salt and pepper. Crush garlic cloves with a rock (leave the papery skin on) and place the cloves together with the herbs around the celeriac. Wrap the foil tightly. Place the parcel among the campfire coals and leave to cook for a minimum of three hours.

3 Remove the foil, squeeze the garlic cloves out of their skins and rub the celeriac with the garlic puree. Place the bulb without the aluminium foil on the barbecue grill and place the lid on (use a big pan if your barbecue doesn't have a lid). Leave to cook for another five minutes.

4 Make the sauce right before serving. Fry the mustard on medium heat in a dry frying pan for about three minutes so it loses its acidity. Keep stirring so the mustard doesn't stick to the bottom of the pan and burn. Add white wine and continue stirring. Season with salt and pepper and allow the sauce to simmer on high heat for a couple of minutes. Stir in the whipped cream and cook for a few minutes. Keep stirring and make sure the sauce doesn't burn.

5 Remove the celeriac from the barbecue and cut into thick slices. Pour the sauce over top and sprinkle with the chopped herbs.

✱ Serve with the remaining sauvignon blanc. This is a great combination!

Arroz arroz

RICH RICE SALAD

INGREDIENTS FOR THE DRESSING
+ 3 tbsp (40 ml / 1¼ fl oz) olive oil
+ 1 tbsp (15 ml ½ fl oz) lemon juice
+ 1 tsp (7 g / ⅛ oz) honey
+ salt and pepper

INGREDIENTS FOR THE SALAD
+ 250 g (6 oz / 1⅕ cups) cooked rice
+ 100 g (3½ oz / ½ cup) peas or green beans (from a tin or jar)
+ 1 big beefsteak tomato, diced
+ 1 onion, finely diced
+ 1 small tin of corn, rinsed and drained
+ 2 tins of sardines (or another canned fish), deboned, cut into pieces
+ 100 g (3½ oz / ½ cup) pitted black olives

Opened packets of rice and pasta are a nuisance when on the road so we cook the whole packet in one go. We use whatever is leftover in a salad the next day. This is also handy when you end up in a spot where having a fire is prohibited. With the pre-cooked rice or pasta ready to go, all you have to do is chop up some ingredients and you have a fully-fledged meal.

METHOD

1 First make the dressing. Mix the oil, lemon juice and honey well, and season with salt and pepper.

2 Combine all salad ingredients with the dressing and your meal is ready!

❋ You can also use the dressing from Salad in a jar (see p. 52).

Chicken kebab

WITH ORANGE MARINADE

INGREDIENTS

+ 1 large tbsp (22 g / ¾ oz) orange marmalade
+ 3 tbsp (40 ml / 1¼ fl oz) olive oil
+ 1 tsp (5 g / ⅛ oz) smoked paprika powder
+ 1 tsp (5 g / ⅛ oz) chilli flakes
+ 2 tsp (10 g / ¼ oz) cumin, crushed
+ 1 tsp (5 g / ⅛ oz) fennel seeds, crushed

+ 4 chicken thighs, skinless and deboned, of equal sizes
+ 1 large onion, in wedges
+ 1 orange, in slices
+ 2 oranges, halved
+ salt and pepper
+ handful of chopped parsley or coriander (cilantro)

Because the sugars in the orange caramelise with the heat of the barbecue, they become even richer in taste. Delicious! Grilled slices of orange are also great to add flavour to a gin and tonic.

METHOD

1 Combine the marmalade with the olive oil and spices to make a marinade, and add the pieces of chicken. Marinate for at least one hour.

2 Light the barbecue and wait until the coals glow.

3 Halve the orange slices. Thread and alternate the pieces of chicken, with the onion wedges and orange slices (folded in half) on four skewers. Sprinkle with salt and pepper.

4 Grill the kebabs on the barbecue until cooked. Place the orange halves on the barbecue and roast until grill marks appear.

5 Sprinkle with chopped herbs and drizzle with juice of the grilled orange.

Delicious with the fennel salad (see p. 95).

TIP
Use a cast-iron pan if you don't have a Dutch oven.

Catalan stew

INGREDIENTS
+ olive oil
+ 4 large chicken thighs (skin on, with bone)
+ 250 g (8 oz / 1½ cups) chorizo, cut into cubes
+ 2 red onions, in wedges
+ 2 cloves of garlic, chopped
+ 1 leek, washed and cut in pieces
+ 1 red capsicum (pepper), in large chunks
+ 200 ml (6¾ fl oz / ⅞ cup) white wine
+ 400 ml (13¼ oz / 1¾ cups) canned, diced tomatoes
+ 250 ml (8½ fl oz / 1 cup) chicken stock
+ 1 tsp (5 g / ⅛ oz) smoked paprika powder
+ 50 g (1¾ oz / ¼ cup) dried apricots, in pieces
+ zest of ½ an orange
+ 2 sprigs of thyme
+ handful of green olives, sliced
+ 400 g (14 oz / 1¾ cups) chickpeas (tin or jar), rinsed and drained
+ 2 tbsp (30 g / 1 oz) chopped flat-leaf parsley
+ salt and pepper

Cooking a stew above a fire is not only fun, it also smells delicious. An added bonus of this one-pot meal is that you don't have much washing up to do. The combination of all these ingredients in one single pot is simply delectable!

METHOD

1 Make a good fire and keep it going for as long as the stew is on.

2 Add a drizzle of olive oil in a pot or Dutch oven and hang from the campfire tripod above the fire. Fry the chicken thighs until brown. Remove the chicken from the pan and set aside.

3 Fry the chorizo in the same pan. Add onion, garlic, leek and capsicum (pepper) and fry for several minutes. Add the wine to the pan.

4 Stir the diced tomatoes and stock in the pot and add paprika powder, orange zest, apricots and thyme. Give a good stir and wait until the mixture simmers. Add the chicken back in and cover with a lid.

5 Simmer for approximately 40 minutes. The chicken should be cooked tender until it falls off the bone. Add the chickpeas and olives and slow-cook.

6 Season with salt and pepper, and sprinkle with parsley before serving. Eat with fresh, crispy bread and butter.

Panzanella
WITH ROASTED VEGETABLES

» **BARBECUE / FIRE** » **PREPARATION IS LONGER THAN ½ HOUR** » **SERVES 4** » **SIDE**

INGREDIENTS
+ 1 loaf stale bread (ciabatta or baguette)
+ olive oil
+ coarse sea salt and pepper
+ 1 yellow capsicum (pepper), de-seeded, cut into big pieces
+ 1 zucchini (courgette), in slices
+ 1 red onion, in wedges
+ 2 cloves of garlic, in slices
+ 8 ripe tomatoes, in big pieces
+ 1 tbsp (15 g / ½ oz) capers, rinsed and drained
+ 100 g (3½ oz / ½ cup) olives
+ 60 g (2 oz / ½ cup) grated parmesan cheese
+ red or white wine vinegar
+ 1 bunch of basil
+ 1 ball of burrata or mozzarella cheese

EQUIPMENT
+ aluminium foil

**Another recipe to use up your old bread.
Throwing out bread really isn't necessary!**

METHOD

1 Light the barbecue or a fire and wait until the coals/wood smoulder.

2 Break the bread into pieces, add to the roasting pan, drizzle with olive oil and sprinkle with coarse salt. Place the roasting pan among the coals for about 10 minutes and toss occasionally.

3 Add the red onion, capsicum (pepper), zucchini (courgette) and garlic on a piece of aluminium foil. Drizzle with a bit of oil and sprinkle with salt and pepper.

4 Wrap up the foil and place the packet in smouldering coals for approximately 10 minutes. Remove with tongs and let it cool down.

5 Add the roasted vegetables, tomatoes and bread in a bowl and mix. Scatter the capers, olives and parmesan cheese on the salad and add with a drizzle of oil and vinegar to taste. Top with basil and burrata/mozzarella.

Holy Kauwboy beans

WITH TOMATO SAUCE AND BACON

» BARBECUE » PREPARATION IS LONGER THAN ½ HOUR » SERVES 4 » DINNER

INGREDIENTS
+ 1 knob of butter
+ 2 slices of smoked pork belly (bacon)
+ 1 loaf of bread, in thick slices
+ 1 red onion, in wedges
+ 2 cloves of garlic, chopped
+ thyme leaves, from 2 sprigs
+ 1 tbsp (15 g / ½ oz) tomato puree
+ 1 tbsp (13 g / ½ oz) brown sugar

+ 50 ml (1¾ fl oz / ¼ cup) balsamic vinegar
+ 500 ml (17 oz / 2 cups) passata (tomato puree)
+ 600 g (1 lb 5 oz / 4 cups) white beans (tin or jar), drained and rinsed
+ salt and pepper
+ 1 sprig of rosemary

This is a cool Holy Kauwboy dish – white beans in tomato sauce with delicious toast.

METHOD

1 Light the barbecue.

2 Melt a knob of butter in a cast-iron pan on the barbecue and fry the bacon until crispy. Remove from the pan and place on a plate.

3 Brush the slices of bread with the bacon grease from the pan and make sure some grease is left in the pan. Fry the onion wedges for approximately five minutes in the leftover grease. Add garlic and thyme leaves and fry for one minute. Add the tomato puree while stirring and fry for about one minute. Add the sugar and balsamic vinegar. Pour in the passata, bring the sauce to the boil and simmer for five minutes. Add the beans toward the very end and cook until heated through. Season with salt and pepper.

4 Toast the slices of bread on both sides on the barbecue grill until crunchy. You could sprinkle with coarse sea salt.

5 Crumble the fried bacon over the white beans in tomato sauce and serve with the toast. Garnish with a sprig of rosemary.

Vegetable parcels

DONE IN DIFFERENT WAYS

» BARBECUE » PREPARATION IS LONGER THAN ½ HOUR » SERVES 2 » DINNER

Food prepared in wrapped aluminium foil or baking paper is referred to as 'en papillote'. The important thing about mastering this cooking method is to seal the parcels so moisture is locked in and the food steams. If you want to combine different types of vegetables, make sure the cooking time is the same for all vegetables. Otherwise half the vegetables could end up being undercooked or overcooked, which is no good.

METHOD

Add some vegetables and seasoning to a sheet of aluminium foil, wrap securely and place on the barbecue.

Some great combinations are:
+ carrot with a drizzle of white wine, cumin, salt and pepper
+ green asparagus with spinach leaves, feta and balsamic vinegar
+ corn, full-cream butter, lime juice, chipotle pepper and salt
+ eggplant (aubergine) with garlic, Middle Eastern spice mix and olive oil
+ beetroot, parsnip, carrot and green herbs with red wine vinegar (see photo)
+ zucchini (courgette), capsicum (pepper), mint and lemon juice

Season the cooked vegetables with salt and pepper, and optionally with finely-chopped herbs.

❋ The cooking time will depend on the type and size of the vegetables and the barbecue temperature; a carrot will take longer to cook than a zucchini (courgette). Make sure you check every now and then to see if the vegetables are cooked.

TIP
*Serve with grilled chicken
pieces or chicken skewers for a
complete meal.*

Super-quick Indonesian salad

WITH POTATOES AND PEANUTS

» **FIRE** » **PREPARATION IS LESS THAN ½ HOUR** » **SERVES 4** » **DINNER**

INGREDIENTS
+ olive oil
+ 1 onion, finely diced
+ 1 capsicum (pepper), finely diced
+ ½ packet of Indonesian spice mix (like bumbu) (50 g / 1¾ oz / ¼ cup)
+ 4 large baked potatoes
+ 1 small tin of peas, rinsed and drained
+ 2 spring onions (scallions), in rings
+ salt and pepper
+ 2 tbsp (30 g / 1 oz) salted peanuts, chopped or crushed with a rock
+ 1 tbsp (15 g / ½ oz) chopped chives
+ sambal (optional)

If you bake potatoes on the smouldering fire in the evening, you'll have half of this dish ready for the next day. When we are on the road we use a ready-made bumbu spice paste. You can use the leftover bumbu the next day to make a nasi-like dish.

METHOD

1 Lightly fry the onion in a bit of oil. Add the capsicum (pepper) and fry for a bit. Add the bumbu and fry for four minutes while stirring.

2 Add the (warm) baked potatoes in a bowl and mash coarsely with a fork. Stir in the bumbu mixture, peas and spring onions.

3 Season with salt and pepper and optionally some sambal if you like it spicy. You can add a drizzle of olive oil if the potato salad is a bit dry.

4 Sprinkle the salad with chopped peanuts and chives.

6 x skewers

MEAT AND VEGETABLES

» BARBECUE » PREPARATION IS OVER 1 HOUR » SERVES 4 » DINNER

Skewers are always a good idea because the combination possibilities are endless. Below are our favourite combinations. So indulge with these beautiful combinations. All recipes are for four people.

Hamburger bun skewer

+ 1 baguette, in 12 slices
+ 1 red onion, cut into 8 wedges
+ 12 small meatballs, approximately 30 g (1 oz / ¼ cup), seasoned for taste
+ 8 small cherry tomatoes
+ ½ zucchini (courgette), cut lengthways in thin slices
+ 4 slices of bacon

Thread a piece of bread, onion wedge, meatball, tomato, zucchini (courgette) slice and bacon onto a skewer. Repeat this twice until the skewer is full. Grill on a barbecue with medium fire and turn regularly until cooked.

Garlic toast skewer

+ 1 stale baguette, cut into cubes of 3 cm (1 inch)
+ 20 g (¾ oz / ¼ cup) butter
+ 2 cloves of garlic, finely chopped
+ coarse sea salt

Melt the butter and fry the garlic. Add the bread cubes in the pan and toss until they are evenly coated with butter. Thread the bread cubes on the skewers. Roast on a barbecue grill on medium heat and turn regularly until the bread is golden brown and crispy.

Ratatouille skewer

+ 4 tbsp (53 ml / 1¾ fl oz) olive oil
+ 1 tbsp (15 ml / ½ fl oz) red wine vinegar
+ 1 clove of garlic, finely chopped
+ 1 tbsp (15 ml / ½ oz) honey
+ salt and pepper
+ 1 eggplant (aubergine), in long thin slices
+ 1 red capsicum (pepper), de-seeded and cut into equal parts
+ 1 red onion, chopped
+ 12 baby potatoes, pre-cooked
+ 12 cherry tomatoes

Make a marinade of oil, vinegar, garlic, honey, salt and pepper and add the vegetables to marinate for 15 minutes. Thread and alternate all vegetables on the skewers. Grill on the barbecue on medium heat and turn regularly until cooked.

Sausage skewers

+ 3 tbsp (40 ml / 1¼ fl oz) olive oil
+ 1 tbsp (15 ml / ½ oz) honey
+ 1 clove of garlic, finely chopped
+ 1 tbsp (15 g / ½ oz) baharat (or other spice mix)
+ 4 sausages, each in 3 pieces
+ 1 capsicum (pepper), de-seeded, cut into coarse pieces
+ 1 red onion, in wedges
+ salt and pepper

Make a marinade of oil, honey, garlic and spices, and stir the sausage, capsicum (pepper) and onion in. Marinate for at least one hour (longer is better). Thread and alternate the sausage, capsicum (pepper) and onion on the skewers. Grill on the barbecue on medium heat and turn regularly until the sausage is cooked. Season to taste with salt and pepper.

Asian beef–mango skewer

+ juice of 1 lime
+ 1 tbsp (15 ml / ½ oz) honey
+ 4 tbsp (60 ml / 2 fl oz) soy sauce
+ 1 red chilli pepper, cleaned, finely chopped
+ 400 g (14 oz) beef steak, cut into 20 even cubes
+ 1 mango, in wedges
+ 4 spring onions (scallions), in pieces of 5 cm (2 inches)
+ black pepper

Make a marinade of lime juice, honey, soy sauce and red chilli pepper, and add the beef cubes. Marinate for at least one hour (longer is better). Thread and alternate the meat, mango and spring onions (scallions) on the skewers. Grill on a barbecue on medium heat and turn regularly until the meat is cooked. Sprinkle with black pepper before serving.

Sweet skewers

+ 8 strawberries
+ 8 marshmallows
+ 1 mango, in 8 pieces
+ handful of chopped mint leaves

Thread and alternate the fruit and marshmallows on a skewer and roast on the barbecue until the marshmallows are browning and start to puff up. Sprinkle with chopped mint.

- 129 -

One-pot pasta
WITH TOMATO, GARLIC AND PECORINO

» FIRE » PREPARATION IS LESS THAN ½ HOUR » SERVES 4 » DINNER

INGREDIENTS
+ 200 g (7 oz / 1 cup) spaghetti
+ 250 g (9 oz / 1 cup) small tomatoes, halved
+ 1 onion, in wafer-thin rings
+ 2 cloves of garlic, minced
+ ½ red chilli pepper, de-seeded and finely chopped
+ handful of fresh basil, torn roughly

+ 2 tbsp (27 ml / 1 fl oz) olive oil
+ 600 ml (20½ fl oz / 2½ cups) water or stock
+ 50 g (1¾ oz / ¼ cup) grated pecorino
+ 100 g (3½ oz / 3⅓ cups) rocket (arugula)
+ salt and pepper

Peckish perfection! Everything in a single pot and done in only 10 minutes.

METHOD

1 Add the spaghetti, tomato, onion, garlic, red pepper and half of the basil into a deep pot and pour oil over. Add the water (or use stock for more flavour).

2 Bring the water to the boil and stir regularly. The pasta should be ready in nine minutes and the water will change into a thick sauce. Add the remaining basil with the pecorino and rocket (arugula), and season with salt and pepper.

❋ Add some fried chorizo or finely-sliced ham before serving.

If the spaghetti doesn't fit in a pan, you can just break it in half.

So much world, so little time

Ideally, we'd spend the whole holiday snacking and having drinks. It's not about the alcohol but more about those delicious nibbles. It's even cosier around a crackling campfire. With these recipes you'll make road-trip friends in no time.

cozy CAMPFIRE MOMENTS

Hotdog on a stick

WITH MUSTARD OR PESTO

» FIRE » PREPARATION IS LONGER THAN ½ HOUR » SERVES 4 » SNACK

INGREDIENTS
+ 8 hotdogs or sausages
+ 1 packet of bread mix (or leftover dough)

+ mustard
+ pesto

We couldn't possibly leave these out. These are at their best with quality chipolata sausages from the local butcher. Don't worry about making the dough from scratch for this recipe; you can also buy a bread mix. Or you can use the leftover dough from the tinned bread recipe (see p. 19).

METHOD

1 Prepare the dough according to the packet instructions. Leave the dough to rise and search the campgrounds for a number of long but solid sticks.

2 Make a fire.

3 Divide the bread dough into eight even parts and roll into long rope-like shapes that can be wrapped around the sausages.

4 Carefully roll the bread dough around the sausages to create a spiral.

5 Carefully but firmly insert a stick into each sausage. Hold over the fire and keep turning until the dough is nice and brown, and the sausages are cooked.

✳ Rub the inside of the dough with mustard or pesto before wrapping it around the sausage. Wrapping a slice of bacon around the sausage before twisting the bread around it is another tasty option.

Strawberry mango salsa

WITH RED ONION AND BASIL

» **PREPARATION IS LESS THAN ½ HOUR** » **SERVES 1** » **PARTY SNACK**

INGREDIENTS
+ 1 large ripe mango, cubed
+ 10 strawberries, chopped
+ 1 red onion, finely diced
+ ½ red chilli pepper, de-seeded, finely chopped

+ handful of torn basil leaves
+ juice of ½ lime
+ 1 tbsp (13 ml / ½ fl oz) olive oil
+ salt and pepper

Great as a bread topping for lunch with a piece of grilled chicken, or as a bruschetta party snack.

METHOD

1 Combine all ingredients in a bowl and season with salt and pepper. Allow to sit so all flavours get absorbed.

Flower wine

WITH STRAWBERRIES AND ROSEWATER

» PREPARATION IS LONGER THAN ½ HOUR » MAKES 1 JUG » DRINK

INGREDIENTS
+ 1 bottle of cooled sparkling white wine or prosecco
+ 180 ml (6 fl oz / ¾ cup) vodka
+ 1 punnet (250 g / 1 cup) strawberries, with tops cut off and halved
+ 4 tbsp (60 ml / 2 fl oz) rosewater

+ 2 tbsp (25 g / 1 oz) granulated sugar
+ edible wild flowers like elderflowers, daisies, chamomile and rose petals
+ handful of ice cubes (if at hand or you can buy them at the local camping convenience store or bar)

Summer solstice is very special to us. It is delightful to enjoy the light and the longest day of the year. Instead of a crown of flowers, we came up with this flower wine. After a couple of glasses of this wine, you'll be dancing around the maypole with ease. Prepare this drink and let the flavours blend while you set up camp.

METHOD

1 Combine all ingredients in a big jug and stir well. Allow to sit for 30 minutes in a cool place so that the flavours mix and blend, and serve with ice cubes.

✱ Some flowers that are safe to eat are: chamomile, violets, marigolds, cornflowers, lavender, East Indian cherries, daisies and dandelions.

When we pick wild flowers, herbs or berries we use the golden rule to only pick what we can carry.

Coconut watermelon
WITH LIME AND MINT

» PREPARATION IS LONGER THAN ½ HOUR » MAKES 1 JUG » DRINK

INGREDIENTS
+ ½ watermelon cut into triangles (with or without skin)
+ 1 litre (34 fl oz / 4¼ cups) cooled coconut water
+ juice of 1 lime
+ bunch of fresh mint
+ handful of ice (from the local supermarket, camping or convenience store)

**Refreshing, thirst-quenching and healthy.
Watermelon adds a lot of flavour but also absorbs flavour.**

METHOD

1 Combine all ingredients in a large jug. Allow to sit for 30 minutes in a cool place so that the flavours mix and blend, and serve with ice cubes.

2 Make sure that each glass you pour has a slice of watermelon, which you can fish out later and eat with your hands.

✻ Add a splash of gin or vodka for adults.

Flavoured butters

Everybody is familiar with the humble herb butter but there are many other ways to flavour butter. A flavoured butter is delicious in aluminium parcels with baked potato, or on grilled fish or meat. Here are a few of combinations.

INGREDIENTS
+ each recipe requires 150 g (5½ oz / 1 cup) soft full-cream butter

Lemon–cumin

Mix 2 tbsp (30 g / 1 oz) of chopped flat-leaf parsley, 1 tbsp (15 ml / ½ fl oz) of lemon juice, 1 tsp (5 g / ⅛ oz) of ground cumin, ½ tsp (2½ g) of paprika powder and ¼ tsp chilli powder with the butter. Season with salt and pepper. Store in a cool place and allow to harden. Delicious with white fish, chicken, turkey, zucchini (courgette) and capsicum (pepper).

Tomato–basil

Mix 2 tbsp (30 g / 1 oz) of chopped basil, 8 finely chopped sundried tomatoes, black pepper and a pinch of salt in with the butter. Store in a cool place and allow to harden. Great with barbecue-roasted vegetables and with a risotto.

Chipotle

Mix the butter with 1 tsp (5 g / ⅛ oz) of chipotle pepper, 3 tbsp (45 g / 1½ oz) of chopped mint leaves, zest of ½ lime and some lime juice. Store in a cool place and allow to harden.

Olives

Stir 2 tbsp (30 g / 1 oz) of chopped olives, 1 tbsp (15 g / ½ oz) of finely-chopped flat-leaf parsley, 4 finely-chopped sundried tomatoes, some lemon juice and pepper through the soft butter. Store in a cool place and allow to harden.

Orange–cinnamon

Stir 2 tsp (10 g / ¼ oz) of cinnamon powder, juice and zest of ½ an orange, and a pinch of salt in with the butter. Store in a cool place and allow to harden. Delicious with barbecued fruit.

Honey-mustard

Stir 1 tsp (5 g / ⅛ oz) of spicy mustard, 2 tsp (14 g / ½ oz) of honey, zest of ½ lime and a pinch of salt in with the butter. Store in a cool place and allow to harden. Tasty with roasted pork.

Tarragon–fennel

Stir 2 tbsp (30 g / 1 oz) of chopped tarragon and ½ tbsp (7 g / ⅛ oz) of crushed fennel seeds in with the butter. Add some lemon juice to taste and season with black pepper and salt. Store in a cool place and allow to harden. Delicious with grilled prawns.

Olive–orange

Mix 2 tbsp (30 g / 1 oz) of chopped green olives, zest of ½ orange, 2 tbsp (30 ml / 1 fl oz) of orange juice, 1 tsp (6 g / ⅛ oz) of coarse sea salt and 1 finely-chopped spring onion (scallion) in with the butter. Store in a cool place and allow to harden.

I want to go on adventures with you.

Oysters

SALTY, BRINY BLISS!

» **BARBECUE** » **PREPARATION IS LESS THAN ½ HOUR** » **SERVES 4** » **PARTY SNACK**

Once we drove to Bretagne in France to knock fresh oysters off the rocks and slurp them down on the spot, with our feet still in the wet sand. We used the leftover oysters on the barbecue that evening.

Oysters with garlic and lemon

INGREDIENTS
+ soft full-cream butter
+ 1 clove of garlic, minced
+ flat-leaf parsley
+ zest and juice of 1 lemon
+ fresh oysters (3 per person is a good measure)
+ pepper

METHOD

1 Combine all ingredients, except the oysters, in a bowl and mix with a fork.

2 Open the oysters and scrub off any debris and sand. Spread the garlic butter on the oysters, place them on the barbecue and cover with a lid. You can place a pan upside down on the barbecue if you don't have a lid, it works just as well.

3 The oysters are ready when the butter is nice and hot but not brown. Season to taste with pepper.

✻ Butter left over? Spread on baguette slices and place on the barbecue.

Oysters with soy sauce, spring onion (scallion) and sushi ginger

INGREDIENTS
+ soy sauce
+ sushi-ginger, finely chopped
+ 1 spring onion (scallion), sliced into thin rings
+ fresh oysters
+ pepper
+ roasted sesame seeds

METHOD

1 Open the oysters and scrub off any debris and sand. Drizzle each oyster with some soy sauce and ginger.

2 Place oysters on the barbecue and cover with a lid. You can place a pan upside down on the barbecue if you don't have a lid. The oysters should be ready in three to five minutes.

3 Remove from the barbecue, scatter spring onion (scallion) on top and garnish with pepper and sesame seeds.

✻ *Tasty:* heat a bit of sesame oil until very hot and pour over the oysters right before serving.

Stuffed bread

WITH BRIE AND ROSEMARY

» **BARBECUE / FIRE** » **PREPARATION IS LESS THAN ½ HOUR** » **SERVES 4** » **SNACK**

INGREDIENTS
+ 1 loaf of bread, whole
+ 2 tbsp (30 g / 1 oz) jam
+ 1 wedge of brie (200 g / 7 oz), in slices
+ 5 sprigs of rosemary

EQUIPMENT
+ aluminium foil

When we're on holiday, we love the morning walks to find the local bakery. You can often find it by just following your nose. The bread is often almost gone by the time we get back to the breakfast table. But if it does survive the way back, what follows below is a great recipe.

METHOD

1 Light the barbecue or make a fire.

2 Make slices in the loaf, about 1 cm (½ inch) apart, making sure not to cut all the way through.

3 Fill the gaps you've made with some jam, a slice of brie and some rosemary. Wrap the bread tightly in aluminium foil.

4 Place above a smouldering fire for approximately 10 minutes until the inside is completely warm and the brie is melted. Check every now and then.

Instant hummus

WITH MASHED CHICKPEAS

» **PREPARATION IS LESS THAN ½ HOUR** » **SERVES 2** » **SNACK**

INGREDIENTS

+ 400 g (14 oz / 1½ cups) canned chickpeas, drained
+ 2 cloves of garlic, crushed with a rock or finely chopped
+ 2 tbsp (30 ml / 1 oz) tahini
+ 1 tsp (5 g / ⅛ oz) cumin powder
+ juice of ½ a lemon
+ 4 tbsp (53 ml / 1¾ fl oz) olive oil
+ salt and pepper
+ paprika powder

Great for breakfast on a slice of bread, for lunch with a salad or as a dip to accompany drinks. Hummus is always a delicious option. At home we use a food processor, but that's not usually possible when travelling, so we made this version. Buy a tin of chickpeas, rinse them clean and add the remaining ingredients to the mix. Mash, spread, eat and enjoy!

METHOD

1 Drain the chickpeas and put them back in the tin. Mash them with a fork (watch out for those sharp edges on the tin).

2 Add the garlic, tahini and cumin and stir well.

3 Add the oil gradually until the hummus has the right consistency.

4 Add lemon juice to taste.

5 Season with salt and pepper and sprinkle with paprika powder.

Mezze without washing up

It's not always possible to wash up a pile of dishes when you're on the road. That's why it's a good idea to use your camping kitchenware and crockery mindfully. We came up with some quick 'dish-washing-free recipes' to make delicious snacks. These also go well with a meal. All recipes make 1 serve.

Strawberry party bread roll

+ 1 small baguette or bread roll, cut open
+ 2 tbsp (30 g / 1 oz) ricotta cheese
+ handful of strawberries
+ balsamic vinegar
+ 4 basil leaves, torn roughly
+ black pepper

Scoop the ricotta onto the baguette and distribute the strawberries. Gently mash flat with a fork. Carefully drizzle with balsamic vinegar, sprinkle with basil and top with some black pepper.

Avocado–tomato crostini

+ 1 small bread roll, in thick slices
+ 1 ripe avocado
+ 1 tbsp (15 ml / ½ fl oz) lemon juice
+ salt and pepper
+ handful of cherry tomatoes, halved
+ piece of feta
+ olive oil

Halve the avocado, remove the stone (pit), slice the flesh diagonally and mash in its shell with lemon juice, salt and pepper. Spread the avocado mix on the bread, top with the tomatoes and carefully mash with a fork. Crumble the feta on each slice of bread and drizzle with olive oil.

Pea–yoghurt dip

+ 1 small tin of green peas
+ 1 tbsp (15 ml / ½ oz) thick yoghurt
+ 1 clove of baked garlic (see p. 99) or 1 small, raw clove
+ 1 tbsp (15 g / ½ oz) chopped mint
+ 1 tbsp (15 g / ½ oz) grated parmesan cheese
+ salt and pepper

Drain and rinse the peas. Finely mash inside the tin and stir in the thick yoghurt, garlic, chopped mint, parmesan cheese and some salt and pepper. Nice with toasted bread or in a salad.

Campfire nachos

INGREDIENTS
+ 1½ tbsp (12 g / ¼ oz) full-cream butter
+ ½ tbsp (7 ml / ⅛ fl oz) olive oil
+ 2 cloves of garlic, pressed
+ 100 ml (3½ fl oz / ⅜ cup) cream
+ 100 ml (3½ fl oz / ⅜ cup) milk
+ 75 g (2¾ oz / ⅔ cup) parmesan cheese
+ salt and pepper
+ red chilli flakes, to taste

+ 1 bag of tortilla chips
+ 1 onion, finely diced
+ 75 g (2¾ oz / ⅔ cup) chorizo, in cubes
+ 50 g (1¾ oz / ¼ cup) pitted black olives, in slices
+ 1 capsicum (pepper), in cubes
+ 1 spring onion (scallion), in rings
+ 75 g (2¾ oz / ⅔ cup) grated cheese

This nacho pizza with chips for a crust is superb! You can literally top it with anything. Also handy for when you're on the go and need to finish up your leftover vegetables, meat and fish from the last meal.

METHOD

1 Make a good fire.

2 Melt the butter with the olive oil in a pan and gently fry the garlic.

3 Add cream and milk and bring to the boil while stirring.

4 Add the parmesan, chilli flakes and salt and pepper, and simmer and stir to a sauce consistency. Remove from the fire.

5 Put the tortilla chips in a cast-iron pan and pour the sauce over. Scatter the remaining ingredients over the chips and top with cheese. Put the pan on the fire. Warm up with the lid on for five to 10 minutes until the cheese is melted and the vegetables are warm.

❋ Distribute the ingredients over and between the tortilla chips so you can taste all the flavours with each bite.

Index

Thanks!

We have worked on this book with much love and pleasure. We are so proud that Road Trip Cooking has been translated into English and is being published in Australia, UK and USA. Excited that our daughter's partner and in-laws who live in the UK can now read our book too. Many thanks to Hardie Grant for your confidence in our book.Thinking up recipes, testing them out, writing the text, but also organising the photo shoots and managing the styling. An intensive yet unique and inspiring undertaking, which is both a learning experience and a project we take great pleasure in completing. Once again we had a fascinating journey and got to relive some beautiful holiday memories.

Despite the fact that we are always together and work long and intensive hours, it was fantastic to note that we complement one another so wonderfully. We feel grateful for every day that we got to go on this adventure together.

Another book, *Annemarieke* and *Claudette*. We love working with you, thank you for believing in us!

Esther, you did it again. You knocked our socks off with your fantastic work. Thanks so much again!

And *Liesbeth* and *Jan*, thank you very much for your hospitality, help and joined brainstorming. Even though our toes nearly froze off from the cold, we enjoyed your company, your beautiful forest, the warm fires and the cozy lunches. A big kiss for you both!

Simone, we found it incredibly fun and inspiring to work with you again. Thanks to you we managed to power on with work. Many thanks!

And of course a very big thank you to our beloved children and grandson. Due to all the chaotic Holy Kauw business we fall behind on our quality time together as a family. But boy oh boy, we always get the party started on the moments that we do spend together. We are so deeply proud of you all and you are alllllwwwaaayyyysss in our thoughts. XOXO

Also a big thanks to *Beanca, Iris, Emma, Laura, Yuan, Lunaworx, Joy Stove* and *Fred*.

Published in 2020 by Hardie Grant Travel,
a division of Hardie Grant Publishing
First published in 2020 by Snor, Utrecht,
Netherlands, *www.uitgeverijsnor.nl*

Hardie Grant Travel (Melbourne)
Building 1, 658 Church Street
Richmond, Victoria 3121

Hardie Grant Travel (Sydney)
Level 7, 45 Jones Street
Ultimo, NSW 2007

www.hardiegrant.com/au/travel

Road Trip Cooking copyright © 2020
Text
The Holy Kauw Company
Photography
Liesbeth Disbergen,
Simone van Rees and Mireille van Elst
Illustrations
Iris Meijering
Design
Esther Snel

Original Edition © 2020
Uitgeverij Snor, Utrecht, Netherlands,
www.uitgeverijsnor.nl

The rights to this book have been negotiated
by Sea of Stories Literary Agency,
www.seaofstories.com,
Sidonie@seaofstories.com

A catalogue record for this
book is available from the
National Library of Australia

Hardie Grant acknowledges the
Traditional Owners of the country on
which we work, the Wurundjeri people of
the Kulin nation and the Gadigal people of
the Eora nation, and recognises their
continuing connection to the land, waters
and culture. We pay our respects to their
Elders past, present and emerging.

Road Trip Cooking
ISBN 9781741177374

10 9 8 7 6 5 4 3 2

Publisher
Melissa Kayser
Project editor
Megan Cuthbert
Translator
Lucy Pijnenburg
Editor
Jessica Smith
Proofreader
Lyric Dodson
Cover design
Murray Batten
Typesetting
Hannah Schubert

Colour reproduction by
Splitting Image Colour Studio

Printed and bound in China by
LEO Paper Products LTD.